FRANCI'S WAR

FRANCI'S WAR

A WOMAN'S STORY OF SURVIVAL

Franci Rabinek Epstein

AFTERWORD BY HELEN EPSTEIN

PENGUIN BOOKS

PENGUIN BOOKS

An imprint of Penguin Random House LLC

penguinrandomhouse.com

Grateful acknowledgment is made to the following:
Page 219 (*bottom*): Photo courtesy of Ronnie Golz
Page 221 (*top left*): Photo courtesy of Doron Leitner
All other photos courtesy of Helen Epstein

Map by Virginia Norey

LIBRARY OF CONGRESS CATALOGING-IN-PUBLICATION DATA

Names: Epstein, Franci, author. | Epstein, Helen, 1947–
Title: Franci's war : a woman's story of survival / Franci Rabinek Epstein ;
afterword by Helen Epstein.
Description: New York : Penguin Books, [2020] |
Identifiers: LCCN 2019039140 (print) | LCCN 2019039141 (ebook) |
ISBN 9780143135579 (paperback) | ISBN 9780525507222 (ebook)
Subjects: LCSH: Epstein, Franci. | Czechoslovakia—History—1938-1945. |
Holocaust, Jewish (1939-1945)—Czechoslovakia—Prague. | Fashion
designers—Czechoslovakia—Prague—Biography. | Theresienstadt
(Concentration camp) | Birkenau (Concentration camp) | Holocaust
survivors—Biography. | Jews—New York (State)—New York—Biography.
Classification: LCC DB2211.E67 A3 2020 (print) | LCC DB2211.E67 (ebook) |
DDC 940.53/18092 [B]—dc23
LC record available at https://lccn.loc.gov/2019039140
LC ebook record available at https://lccn.loc.gov/2019039141

Printed in the United States of America
1 3 5 7 9 10 8 6 4 2

Set in Adobe Garamond Pro
Designed by Cassandra Garruzzo

To Helen, Tommy, and David
In memory of their grandparents

CONTENTS

FRANCI'S WAR

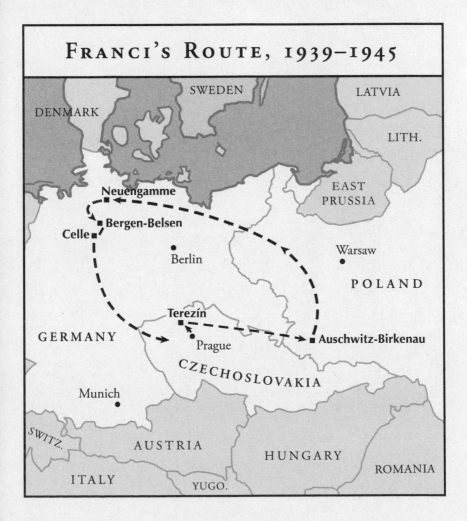

FRANCI'S ROUTE, 1939–1945

SWEDEN

DENMARK

LATVIA

LITH.

EAST
PRUSSIA

Neuengamme

Bergen-Belsen

Celle

Berlin

Warsaw

POLAND

Terezín

GERMANY

Prague

Auschwitz-Birkenau

CZECHOSLOVAKIA

Munich

SWITZ.

AUSTRIA

HUNGARY

ROMANIA

ITALY

YUGO.

1

It was a hot day in the first week of September 1942, and the Industrial Palace of Prague was teeming with people. Most were lying or sitting on the loose straw on the floor; others were wandering around in a stunned daze. Gone were the shiny displays of Czechoslovak industry that had given the place the air of a happy carnival.

I had often come to the Industrial Palace when I was a child and my father's electro-technical firm, Korálek & Rabinek, had a booth.* It had always been a treat. I returned home with free samples, balloons, and stacks of glossy catalogs. This time I would not return home because the Industrial Palace had been converted to the assembly point for the deportation of undesirables, i.e., Jews, by edict of the Nuremberg race laws.

None of us should have been surprised. The trap had been closing

---

* Editor's note: The assembly point was then called Radiopalác Pražských vzorkových veleterhů.

for three years by then, but the systematic humiliation and brain-washing had been gradual and only partially successful. Our humanity was still intact. Our situation had somehow not fully registered until now. It was quite a shock to be suddenly treated like so much cattle.

I was twenty-two and lying with my head in my mother's lap in a sort of stupor. I had just had a tonsillectomy. I had not eaten for a few days and was having trouble breathing the air that was filled with straw dust. My mother kept stroking my hair and trying to make me drink a little water. My father was walking around from one acquaintance to another, hoping to find out what was in store for us. Groups of SS men were storming in and out, yelling orders and rounding up groups of Jewish men to clean the latrines. They made a point of picking out the most distinguished-looking older men in the crowd, the men wearing glasses. My father was one of them.

When they told me in the hospital that my parents and I had been called up for a transport, the nurse, who was a friend of ours, said *We can get you out of it because of the surgery*. I thought this over for a few minutes and then said *I'm not letting them go alone. They're too old and they don't have anybody else*. My mother was sixty and my father was sixty-five. I couldn't visualize those two people going alone anywhere. And there was a little egotistical motivation too. My husband was already gone. I would have been left all alone. Besides, by September 1942 I was so fed up with all the restrictions in Prague that I thought any change of scene would be a relief, no matter what was waiting on the other end. I was always like that, unfortunately.

2

Hitler invaded Czechoslovakia on March 15, 1939, a bit over two weeks after I turned nineteen. My interest in politics was nonexistent, and I was only vaguely aware that all four of my grandparents were Jewish. A year earlier, I had become the owner of my mother's *haute couture* business. I was carefree, slightly spoiled, and mainly interested in dancing, my business, flirting, and skiing, in that order.

My father, Emil Rabinek, was born a Jew in Vienna in 1878. He was the youngest son in a family of Austrian civil servants and a firm believer in assimilation. At the age of twenty, he had converted to Catholicism in order to circumvent the *numerus clausus*—the Jewish quota—at the University of Berlin. Emil Rabinek had fought with the Austrian army during the First World War without much enthusiasm, and welcomed the formation of the Czechoslovak Republic in 1918. He had lived in Prague for many years. While he remained—emotionally and culturally—an Austrian, he saw the establishment of the Czechoslovak Republic as a new experiment in social democracy, a sort of Switzerland in the heart of Europe with equal rights for all minorities. He chose to be a Czechoslovak citizen.

The next twenty years justified his choice. My father lived as a member of the German-speaking community of Prague, patronizing German clubs, theaters, and concert halls. One of his favorite statements was *I am a Czechoslovak citizen of German nationality.* He never learned proper Czech. Our extensive library was almost entirely German, with translations from French, English, and Russian literature. He led me to admire everything German or, at least, filtered through the German language. There was not one Czech book in the house until I was in my teens and began to buy them for myself.

Though my father had had plenty of warning about Nazism, he dismissed the news that came from Germany as propaganda. He believed in German decency, justice, honor, and civilization. He was also absolutely certain that Czechoslovakia was a strong country, its sovereignty guaranteed by its French and British allies. Not even the occupation of Austria in March 1938 had shaken his convictions, and he considered his cousins who had fled Vienna to be cowards. His eldest sister, Gisela Rabinek Kremer, and some of her children had remained there. That gave him further evidence that it was a mistake to panic and run.

There were, in addition, financial considerations. In February 1920, when I was born, my father had been a rich man—co-owner of a shipyard and an electro-technical wholesale house. Following the American Crash of 1929 and the depression years, his wealth had shrunk. We still had our beautiful apartment, with all its books and paintings, and were living very comfortably. But by the time the Germans occupied Czechoslovakia, our income came mostly from my mother's and my *haute couture* business, which, in earlier years, he had considered the caprice of a liberated career woman. Now, my father kept busy as its bookkeeper. Business was good, but most of our capital was tied up in it, and not readily available to convert into foreign currency on the black market. My father often said *At our age we are not emigrating without capital.*

Unbeknownst to me and in spite of all his brave talk, my father was writing letters to his cousin in England with the purpose of getting me out of the country. Nothing ever came of it, and only twenty-five years later did I learn from this guilt-ridden relative how my father had pleaded with him to do something, anything, to save me. He must have done it under pressure from my mother, who felt that a major catastrophe had befallen the Czech nation in general and our family in particular.

My mother, Josefa "Pepi" Sachsel, spoke excellent Czech and had a very deep allegiance to the Czech people, although she, too, was born in Vienna. Both her parents had died when she was nine, and in 1891, she and her two older brothers were taken in by Aunt Rosa, her father's sister, and moved to the Czech town of Kolín.

Rosalia Sachsel Lustfeld, according to my mother, was desperately poor and deeply pious. A regular at Kolín's synagogue, she preferred to discuss the Talmud with itinerant Chasidim to running her used clothing store. The brothers soon ran away: Emil Sachsel joined the Austro-Hungarian Navy and eventually settled in Bratislava; Rudolf Sachsel became a peddler and eventually a rich wholesaler in Prague. Pepi, being a girl and only nine, remained in Kolín, learned Czech, attended grammar school, and was stuck with Aunt Rosa's overpowering love, religious fervor, and rigidity. This combination of traits managed, over the years, to sour my mother's connection to observant Judaism and turn her into an agnostic.

The Hilsner Affair was also a factor. In 1899, when Pepi was seventeen, a Czech Catholic seamstress was found dead in a pool of blood during Passover. A Jewish vagrant named Leopold Hilsner was the chief suspect and accused of ritual murder. My mother told me there had been pogroms all over the country, including in Kolín. And another factor that soured her on Judaism: her first love had been a wealthy Jewish boy in Kolín, and his parents had shipped him out of the country to prevent him from marrying a poor orphan.

Aunt Rosa had taught her niece how to assess used clothing and how to sew. At twenty, Pepi followed her brothers' lead and left Kolín. She moved in with her brother Rudolf in Prague and found a job at one of the city's best-known dress shops, Moritz Schiller. Within two years, she became its *directrice* and buyer. My mother had no wish to marry, but to allay Aunt Rosa's fears for her virtue in the big city, she married a former Kolín schoolmate, and became Mrs. Oskar Weigert.

During that first decade of the twentieth century, Pepi traveled to Paris every year and became a sophisticated businesswoman. But her marriage was miserably unhappy because Oskar had syphilis, then an incurable disease. In 1908, she had a nervous breakdown. Her boss conferred with Aunt Rosa and Pepi's prosperous brothers, and they were able to get her marriage annulled on the grounds that it was never consummated. Josefa Weigert moved into a boardinghouse, where she met electrical engineer Emil Rabinek. After a decade-long affair, and the death of Aunt Rosa and his mother, Fanny Rabinek, they married in December 1918.

Emil Rabinek did not object to Pepi's career, but did not want her to work for anyone else. So she opened her own *haute couture* house, Salon Weigert, in a space adjoining their apartment on 53 Spálená in Prague. My mother was equally at home with Czech and German clients, perhaps leaning a little more to the Czech side. Many of them adored her and were often friends as well as customers. She had excellent relations with her Czech employees. I was born in February 1920, and as I grew up, she balanced my father's Germanophilia quite nicely.

My own allegiance was entirely with the Czechoslovak Republic. I was, after all, a child of the Republic, only two years younger than the state itself. I considered myself a Czechoslovak citizen. My parents tried to bring me up as a citizen of the world. German was spoken at home, Czech was spoken everywhere else, and I was sent to Prague's French school, baptized a Catholic, and attended church and confession. I knew I had Jewish family members because I visited Aunt Rosa's grave in the Jewish cemetery once a year with Mutti (my mother). But religion did not interest me very much. By the time I was thirteen, I began to question Catholic dogma and soon afterward asked my father to have my papers changed to read "without religious affiliation."

Those were the kind of Jews I and my parents were when the Germans occupied Prague on March 15, 1939.

3

In April, a tall, sandy-haired man with a Prussian crew cut had appeared at our door and identified himself politely as the commissar appointed by the Reichsprotektor to "aryanize" our Jewish business. After inspecting our records and watching how the workroom operated, he must have come to the realization that our salon was entirely dependent on the taste and work of its owners and their relationship to its customers—not a potential gold mine for him. Hinting broadly that his wife needed new clothes, he advised us off the record to sell the business *pro forma* to one of our employees and perhaps stay on as hired help. After he left, Mutti and I went into the workroom to discuss the situation with our staff. Our seamstresses and one tailor were all under thirty, and our belief in their loyalty was so strong that it never occurred to us to worry about a possible leak to the authorities about the proposition we were about to make to them.

They did not seem to be surprised. This sort of thing was going on all over Prague, but somehow none of us had expected it so soon. A lively discussion began about who should become the *pro forma* owner. We decided to sleep on it. My parents had misgivings about putting our livelihood into the hands of an employee—no matter how loyal—while I thought the idea simple and brilliant. Actually, we had no choice. We could close the business completely, but that would entail living on our savings for an unforeseeable length of time and also deprive more than a dozen people of their jobs.

The next day Marie, who had been working for us the longest, offered to be part of the transaction. A secret contract was drawn up by a reliable attorney and member of the Czech underground who had arranged more than one similar transfer. Marie and I would draw the same salary and divide the profit in half. To make the transaction plausible, the lawyer made a loan to Marie, enabling her to buy the business from us. We repaid him. The contract was buried on the grounds of the attorney's country house. A sign painter changed the names over our entrance door.

After this, life went on more or less unchanged, except that the staff began to call Marie "Miss Marie," instead of by her first name. Our customers, including the German customers, accepted the situation without much comment. Some inquired discreetly whether my mother was getting her fair share.

Then the systematic harassment of the Czechs in general and the Jews in particular began. First came the definition of who was considered a Jew: anyone with at least two Jewish grandparents. I discovered that I had four. Then Jews were barred from public places, and signs to that effect were put up at all restaurants, coffeehouses, playgrounds, swimming pools, theaters, concert halls, etc.: JEWS UNWANTED. Only the river was still accessible to us.

Jews were dismissed from all the universities; Jewish doctors were allowed to treat only Jews, and their offices were confiscated one by one. Eventually all Jewish-owned businesses were aryanized and the National Bar Association disbarred all Jewish lawyers. But some Czech organizations and businesses procrastinated. The Czech Philharmonic resisted the longest, almost one year. The national gymnastic association, Sokol, complied, but a large number of regional groups let it be known privately that its Jewish members were as welcome as before.

We were ordered to wear a yellow star with the word JUDE in the middle. This had to be sewn on the left side of every outer garment, over the heart. Anyone circumventing this order was subject to immediate arrest. My father and I considered this the ultimate insult; Mutti accepted it much more philosophically, maybe as a punishment for our disregard of our ancestry.

Next came the confiscation of all jewelry, which had to be brought to appointed places in person. Then radios. Then Jews were only allowed to ride in the last car of the tram and only allowed to sit in the event that no Aryan was standing. The following year, only Jews who worked and had a special pass could ride the tram. The ones who did not have a pass had to walk everywhere.

There were certainly some Czechs who sympathized with the Germans and who were quite happy about the persecution of the Jews. But most of the Czechs I came into contact with resented these edicts. Some made a point of giving up their seat in the tram to let a Jewish woman sit down. These well-meant gestures led to embarrassing situations at times. Prague was full of Germans in civilian clothes. There were altercations in trams or buses that ended in fistfights if only Czechs were involved, but could get much more unpleasant if a German was present. Meanwhile, the oppressed tried to fight back as best as they could. Uninsured jewelry got stashed away with Aryan friends. Large radios were moved to the homes of non-Jewish neighbors and friends, and smaller, older ones were turned in instead. Many a yellow star was hidden on the street by a strategically carried book or handbag, or often not worn at all.

I did that for a long time and, as an added precaution, decided to get a nose job. My father and some of my Jewish friends had always teased me about having a so-called Jewish nose. I was an avid moviegoer and the prohibition on Jews attending cinemas was one of the hardest for me to bear. If my nose were a different shape and I didn't wear a star, I reasoned, I could pass without much risk. I had the operation and wound up, after four weeks of headaches, looking like my mother with her straight, slightly turned-up nose, but never actually got to go to the movies because she got hysterical every time I even mentioned the idea.

4

In June 1939, my parents and I were arrested by the Gestapo—because of my boyfriend's mother's jewelry. My boyfriend was Pepik "Joe" Solar. His mother had stashed some of her jewelry with a Major Z., who had been Joe's commander in the Czechoslovak Army. Because they were looking for Joe, they arrested us.

This was my first contact with the Gestapo. They arrested my parents first without telling them the charges, and me a few hours later, when I returned home from an errand. They interrogated us separately for twelve hours, with my parents totally unaware of what this was all about. Compared to what would happen later in the war, I was not mistreated during those long hours. I was even offered chocolate and cigarettes, alternating with threats of shooting me or my parents if I didn't talk. That night, I was put in a car with my parents and two Gestapo men. We were taken to Pankrác prison and lined up, facing the wall, with some fifty other people.

My parents were on either side of me. Behind our backs, a few guards were marching up and down. After a while, my father turned toward me with a questioning look. Instantly, he was knocked down by a guard, his glasses flying off his face. I bent down automatically to help him up, but a shouted order stopped me, and I realized that it was better to keep still. By midnight we were all led off to different cells. I was put in with two middle-aged ladies to whom I announced that this was all some terrible mistake and that, clearly, I would be going home in the morning. One of them seemed to find my announcement very amusing, while the other just waved her hand, too depressed to argue with me.

The first woman was named Marianne Golz. She was very attractive, with flaming red hair and the self-assurance of an actress, which it turned out she had been. The second was Ludmila, the wife of a high officer in the Czechoslovak Army and a functionary of Sokol, who had fled the country to join the free Czech soldiers abroad. Ludmila had been imprisoned for the previous three months and repeatedly questioned about the network that enabled Czech men such as her husband to slip out of the country under the noses of the Germans.

My two cellmates could not have been more different from each other. Where one was flamboyant and witty, the other was dignified and quiet. Where one's moral attitudes seemed to be at least questionable, the other had been married for twenty-five years to the same husband with rocklike love and devotion. These involuntary roommates had more in common than I at first understood. They both were instantly protective of me and took it upon themselves to give me an elementary education in the ground rules of German detention.

The first rule of the game seemed to be not to let your interrogators know anything they did not already know. Never admit anything, they told me, especially not the truth. Never volunteer information, no matter what the promise of reward.

To my nineteen-year-old eyes, Marianne seemed like an adventuress and *demi-mondaine* with great sensitivity and compassion for others, an enormously courageous daredevil. Ludmila's courage manifested itself more in quiet passive resistance to her captors. I believe that neither of them ever implicated another person during the entire time they were detained. I learned that Marianne was an early anti-Nazi and a Christian who had been married to a Jewish journalist in Vienna. He had fled Austria in March 1938. Marianne had stayed behind in Vienna, obtained a quick divorce on racial grounds, and went to work to help her friends.

She smuggled their money and jewelry into Switzerland, while carrying on an affair with an SS officer in Vienna. This affair allowed her to cover her tracks and make a fair number of useful connections in the high echelons of the SS, in and out of Austria. It had all worked beautifully until the day when the gentleman was transferred to more important duties. At that point, Marianne prudently decided to move her activities to Prague. Here, she became involved with the Czech Resistance. Unfortunately, one arrest had led to another, someone talked too much, and Marianne wound up as Ludmila's cellmate. Despite all her connections to the SS, she was unable to get word out that she was being held in Pankrác prison.

Fascinated by Marianne's stories and personality, I listened closely to what she reported about the experience of the Jews in Austria and the methods used by the Nazis. We had plenty of time and nothing else to do since day after day went by without any of us being called in for questioning. Marianne explained to me the mechanics of the system of confiscation, humiliation, and—finally— deportations, which had already started in Vienna.

Marianne did not know where exactly these people had been taken, but she did know that the weight of their luggage was limited to fifty kilos, and that everything else one owned had to stay behind. She tried to convince me to try to escape if and when I got out of this prison. She *did* convince me that it was foolish for my family to remain in an apartment adjoining the business where I was employed, not only because of the risk to Marie but because our apartment was large and modern, and would be confiscated sooner or later. We would then be forced into one room in another "Jewish apartment."

All this useful information was spiced with quite incredible stories from her life, some of which caused acute embarrassment to Ludmila, who did not consider them fit for my nineteen-year-old ears. But the two women adamantly agreed that the Nazis were monsters who had to be fought on every level. I began to believe every word they said. Every day, I looked for my mother during the twenty-minute exercise march in the prison yard, but never saw her.

Two weeks later I was called for interrogation and released half an hour later. Much later I would learn that Marianne was released a few weeks after me, when one of her SS friends returned from a trip and did not find her home, but rearrested in 1943, when her luck ran out. She was beheaded in Pankrác prison that year. I never learned what happened to Ludmila.

5

I came home to our empty apartment. My first stop was my father's desk. I opened the top drawer, and found—to my horror—a list of *my* mother's jewelry with Major Z.'s address. I also found a suspicious-looking vial without a label that contained little pills. Then the doorbell rang and I stuck it into my pocket. It was my boyfriend Joe, who filled me in on what had happened while I was in prison.

Joe had contacted a Czech lawyer with access to the Gestapo to find out why we had been arrested. He learned that his brother Paul was suspected of dealing in foreign currency and that two Gestapo agents had searched his apartment. There, they found a slip of paper with Major Z.'s name and address, and notes about jewelry, and locked the brother's family up. Then they interrogated Paul's mother and asked about Joe's whereabouts. She told them that Joe was probably visiting his girlfriend—i.e., me. They arrested us, confronted Major Z., and let him go with an admonition to stop being a Jew-lover. We were released from Pankrác for the sum of twenty thousand Czech crowns, a ransom delivered in a plain envelope, stuck into a copy of *Mein Kampf*. My parents were indeed released a few hours after me.

Each of us reacted to that first imprisonment in a different way. My father was furious at my boyfriend, and ranted about keeping lists that implicated uninvolved others. He stopped only when I produced the list I had found in his desk. Joe drew the conclusion that the Germans could be bought and that his newly found connection to the Gestapo might prove useful in the future. Mutti was happy to see me all in one piece, and ready to forgive everything and everybody.

I told them what I had heard from my cellmate Marianne. They listened but considered me naive: Marianne might have been an *agent provocateur* put in with us to acquire information. Nonetheless, I insisted on discussing her suggestion that we give up our large, centrally located Prague apartment, move the business to a separate location, and look for smaller, less attractive living quarters that would not invite German requisition. My idea was to move to the suburbs, far from the center of town, where raids and other surprises were less likely. It took months to convince my parents, but I stood my ground and we eventually did just that.

When the Second World War officially began on September 1, 1939, my father retreated into a dreamworld of his own, never doubting an Allied victory. He walked six miles every day to listen to the broadcasts of the BBC in the home of one of our employees where our radio was parked. He had maps all over the house with flags pinned into position where the Germans claimed to be and where the BBC said they were. The situation looked bleak, but once the war started, my father's optimism soared sky-high. That Christmas, Joe gave me a puppy. Tommy soon became the center of my family's attention, and a faithful companion during my father's news-gathering walks.

In the beginning of 1940, with the war going into high gear, my boyfriend became deeply involved with the Resistance's clandestine smuggling of former Czechoslovak servicemen out of the country to enable them to join the anti-Nazi military effort abroad. Joe had been discharged from the army only a short time before the occupation. While serving, he had been a happy-go-lucky guy, never taking the army very seriously. After the German occupation, his attitude had changed completely. He felt guilty sending other men off, and by the end of April, he had decided to join the growing units of volunteers.

The exit route had been tested many times before and was considered fairly safe. A patriotic ranger led groups of five to ten men through the woods across the border to Hungary. From there they made their way to Yugoslavia and eventually to Palestine and England, where a Czechoslovak government-in-exile had been formed. There was a long and tearful leave-taking at our house, with even my father moved to sniffles, and Joe left without forgetting to arrange for two baskets of flowers to be delivered the following day for Mutti and me.

After three days without news we were convinced that he had made it safely and felt happy and proud. Then, when I returned home from work a week later, Mutti told me that I had a visitor in the dining room. There was Joe, with a week-old beard, smelling of sweat and manure, a picture of utter misery. Something had gone wrong and his group had been intercepted by a German patrol. Some were caught, some were shot, but Joe and a buddy had escaped and made their way back to Prague on foot, getting rides and food from sympathetic farmers. They had covered about four hundred miles over back roads and fields. There was no way of knowing whether the Germans were looking for them, and it was dangerous to stay at his mother's or even my house. He was even dangerous to the Resistance.

For the next few weeks he disappeared into different mountain cabins owned by his friends, constantly changing his location. Before he left, we decided to get married. I felt terribly sorry for Joe, and also, he now seemed something of a hero to me. I had always liked him for his marvelous sense of humor. No matter how bad things looked, he could always make me laugh. He was my favorite playmate. Besides, Jews now had a curfew of eight p.m., and my parents and the puppy were just not enough company for the twenty-year-old woman I now was.

6

When I broke the news to my parents, my father flew into a rage, accusing Joe of stealing me away from him. Mutti, on the other hand, liked the idea of our getting married, thinking it was good for me to be with another young person in this difficult time. After Joe came out of hiding and returned to Prague, we finally decided to move out of the center of Prague. Our landlord was delighted: this enabled him to rent our apartment quietly to new Czech tenants.

We found a tiny place—just two rooms and a kitchen, with no central heating—on the outskirts of the city next to the film studios in Barrandov. It was far away from everything, but there were fields and woods to walk in. It would not have been bad for a young couple by themselves, but we moved there with my parents so as to avoid requisitioning too much space. Some of our furniture was sold, and the rest crammed into this new apartment. The business was moved to a new location in the center of Prague.

On August 20, 1940, we got married. Jewish marriages were no longer permitted in Prague's beautiful City Hall—only in a small district hall on the outskirts of the city. We were not allowed to ride in taxis anymore, and I refused to go on the tram with the enormous bouquet of white roses that Joe presented me. The problem was solved by asking one of our young apprentices to carry it for me in a shopping bag.

In consideration of the times, I had decided to get married in a simple black dress, but I had an unbelievably silly pale-blue hat that I carried in a paper bag and only put on for the photographer in the waiting room. The little district office was crowded with my staff and friends, and afterward we had a luncheon at Père Louis, a restaurant we had visited regularly during our courtship and whose owner circumvented the anti-Jewish laws simply by closing "for illness."

Our four-day honeymoon took place in Zlín, an ugly, industrial town and home to the Baťa works, simply because this was the only hotel in the country that still admitted Jewish guests. Even there we had to eat in our room because the dining room was off-limits. After those four days, our honeymoon and our privacy were over. We returned to my family's small apartment in Prague, where I was still considered "the child" and my husband was treated like an adopted sibling.

By then, I was the only wage earner in the family. Our former employee Marie had undergone a subtle change over the course of the year. Being the owner of a thriving business had given her a status she had previously only dreamed of. Incessant anti-Semitic propaganda by the occupying forces had given this simple girl an idea of the risks she was taking by continuing to employ my mother and me, and, perhaps, even a justification of our reversed roles. For the moment, the Germans were winning the war and there was not the slightest sign in the air that the status quo could not continue for our lifetimes.

After our move to Barrandov, Marie decided that one Rabinek was enough to keep the old clients coming to the salon. This put my parents out of work. My new husband had not held a regular job since the German occupation. It was a precarious situation. Our savings were disappearing at an alarming rate as we bought food and other necessities on the black market. Czechoslovakia, which had been an exporter of farm products and meat, was now on ration cards, because the occupiers siphoned everything off to the Reich. Jewish ration cards were stamped with a capital *J* and shopping hours restricted to two hours in the late afternoon when there was not much left in the stores.

The value of Czech currency dropped by the day. So did prices for jewelry and art objects, because of the oversupply. Foreign currency skyrocketed. Every morning I pedaled to work on my bicycle, a shoulder bag covering my yellow star, and scanned Marie's face to assess her mood. Would she fire me today? Tomorrow? Next week? When?

Then, six weeks after Joe and I were married, I found myself pregnant. Actually, my mother diagnosed it, claiming that I had a different expression on my face. A check with a doctor proved her correct. My father held forth about the irresponsibility of having children at a time like this and demanded that I have an immediate abortion. For once, I was in total agreement with him. I did not want a baby. I was twenty years old, saddled with responsibility for four people, wanting to amuse myself as much as possible within the constraints of our severely limited way of life. Besides, my husband was such a playmate that the idea of him becoming a father made me laugh.

Joe, of course, was delighted by the news and did not want to understand any arguments against the birth of his child. Mutti became very sentimental: having a grandchild had enormous appeal, but even she had misgivings about the timing. Abortions had always been illegal in Czechoslovakia, but the law was regularly circumvented. The problem now was that Jewish doctors no longer had offices, and Christian physicians were forbidden to see Jewish patients. Joe found a young Czech gynecologist through one of his army buddies to perform the operation, but it had to be done in his office on a Saturday and he could not give me much anesthetic. I had to be in and out as soon as possible. His wife assisted him.

The night before my abortion, Joe's mother died of a heart attack. In spite of that, Joe went with me to the gynecologist's office and pleaded until the last moment for me to change my mind. Afterward, I was bundled into a friend's car and driven home, where Mutti made an inordinate fuss, watching my temperature round the clock. Joe was quite shaken by the events, and I was too wrapped up in myself to realize the trauma he must have gone through. There had never been much love between my mother-in-law and myself. She had always disapproved of me because I was more inter-ested in my business than in Joe's shirts or the kitchen. I could never forgive the stupidity that had led to my parents' ordeal at the hands of the Gestapo. For the sake of appearances, I had to go to the fu-neral two days later and looked so drawn and sick that everyone was surprised at how deeply I seemed to mourn her passing.

7

Life stabilized somewhat, and for a year, we lived a very quiet life, removed from the tensions and rumors of Prague's center. My parents took my puppy, Tommy, for long walks to the city limits; Jews were not permitted to walk beyond them anymore. My father and Joe played chess and kept the war maps up to date. The river was still free, and we went swimming often that summer. There was one café assigned to Jews, where a combo played and where we could dance on a Saturday afternoon. Somehow, we became accustomed to our strictly circumscribed existence. We spent New Year's Eve of 1940 with our Jewish neighbors, two young couples who were still living in their own house, drinking to a speedy end of the war.

Nocturnal visits like these were not very frequent and somewhat risky because diagonally across from our house lived a Sudeten German collaborator named Lachmann, who spent a large part of his time looking out his window and surveying the doings of the four Jewish families living on the street. Because of the curfew, we had to wait for darkness and then walk over in slippers so as not to attract his attention. This self-appointed guard haunted us day and night. He kept track of whether we observed the shopping hours allotted to Jews in our little grocery store. Our puppy was a particular thorn in his eye, and he dropped hints all over the neighborhood that Jews should not be allowed to keep dogs for their pleasure.

In October 1941, we heard about the first deportations of Jews. Only the wealthiest families were taken and sent to Lodz, in occupied Poland. Soon there was news that they were doing all right, and at first, this did not seem the most horrible of fates to us, aside from the inconvenience. To the Jews remaining in Prague, it did not seem too different from being relocated by Nazi orders to the former ghetto, where most Jews now lived one family to one room. We were still safe and forgotten out in the sticks of Barrandov.

But to be on the safe side, Jewish housewives began to bake cookies, hoard sugar and all kinds of fat—just in case. Everyone started dying sheets and pillowcases dark colors so as to save on soap in the uncertain future. We all acquired large duffel bags and knapsacks at black market prices, to be packed within twenty-four hours if necessary. Every time a family member left the house, he or she would carefully carry out a package containing some prized possession—a piece of china, a small rug, or a painting removed from its frame—and take it for safekeeping to a trusted Christian friend. Joe and I carried out our whole library, book by book.

It was a good way to keep busy and prevent us from brooding too much. Strangely enough, I was still working, smiling at our loyal customers, and listening to the German ones assure me repeatedly that they had absolutely no personal animosity toward me or my mother, never forgetting to send her their greetings. Our Czech clients were like rays of sunshine, offering whatever help they could give. Many an heirloom from our house found its way into theirs. They also—very forcefully—kept Marie aware of the fact that I was the reason why they kept coming to the salon. It was those clients and my friends from school and sports that helped me keep my faith in the human race.

Frustrated that I was supporting the entire household, Joe had gotten involved with a group of young men trading foreign currency on the black market to bring home some money. Initial success led to carelessness, and in February 1942, they all got arrested and sentenced to five months in prison, which was bad enough in itself, but made far worse by the assassination of Reichsprotektor Reinhard Heydrich.

In June, after this success of the Czech Resistance, the Nazis went berserk, terrorizing the population, combing the city for the culprits, arresting people by the hundreds, picking prisoners at random every day and gunning them down in the courtyards of jails.

Joe had been able from the start of his term to send me messages via a Czech guard, who proved so reliable that I had even received a four-foot-high white lilac bush for my twenty-second birthday at the end of February. Then, I had been able to visit Joe in prison once a week and bring him food and clean clothes. Now, he bombarded me with pleas to get him out. My father treated these desperate appeals with disdain; he called it "unmanly" to ask a woman for help in such a dangerous situation. In his view Joe only got what he deserved for the risks he had been taking on the black market.

To my constant amazement, my father still accepted German rules and regulations as valid law, if not exactly justice. But all of us were being conditioned to regard the hundreds of absurd decrees as a part of life. Not even the Jews were immune to the incessant barrage of the Nazi propaganda machine.

After the Nazis destroyed the entire town of Lidice in reprisal for the Heydrich assassination, it wasn't so easy to access someone who would take a bribe. I was unable to find anyone who would stick his neck out for Joe during that June of 1942. The constant arguments with my father made me even more tense, and for the first time in my life, I began to stand up to his very often unfair criticisms. Mutti had her hands full trying to maintain family harmony and often wound up as a lightning rod for both of our angers. To make matters even worse, Marie informed me that given the precarious situation, I could no longer set foot in the business. My pride was so hurt that I didn't even ask her for a small amount of money.

At a loss for what to do with the abundance of free time I now had, I began to clean house, waxing and polishing everything in sight. I also learned to cook a little, as much as our severely limited supplies allowed—mainly vegetables. I never again want to eat a carrot cake, or potato goulash, or any of the other concoctions of that time.

Once, having nothing to do, I attached a Star of David to my puppy Tommy's collar, telling him that he was a Jew too. Before we left for our walk, Mutti called after me to take that star off the dog. In the fields, I let him off leash, and he soon disappeared from sight, hunting rabbits. After whistling and calling for him for quite a while, I returned home alone. I wasn't really worried because he used to run around freely and always came back. When he didn't show up by nightfall, all three of us got concerned, but because of the curfew, we had to wait until morning to look for him. We fanned out in different directions. On our return, we found Mutti crying on our doorstep. She had heard that Lachmann had seen the dog and, supposedly mistaking him for a rabbit, shot him. It's callous to admit, but we mourned the dog more than my mother-in-law, and the loss only added to my sense of impending doom. I began to wish for something to happen—anything, just a change.

8

I t came sooner than I expected. In the middle of July, Joe finished his sentence and was released from prison. Two weeks later, the dreaded narrow blue strip of paper was delivered to our door, calling him up for a transport to Terezín. This transport was for young men only. They were to build an extension track from the existing station in Bohušovice to Terezín, the old military garrison built by the Habsburg emperor Joseph II in the eighteenth century and named Theresienstadt for his mother, Empress Maria Theresa.

We were aware of the ongoing transports, and after Joe left, it was clear that our days at home were numbered. But then, oddly, the transports suddenly stopped. This was the reason why we had decided, at long last, that I should have my tonsils removed. I had been putting it off for years simply because I had been too scared.

Father walked downtown to the Jewish community offices where the transport slips were dispatched to find out if there were any transports planned for the next two or three weeks. Assured that there did not seem to be any, I entered the one and only Jewish hospital in Prague in the early morning. I was operated on at eight, under local anesthetic, but the doctor ran into some snags and this ostensible triviality lasted almost two hours. I was asleep when in the afternoon a friend of Joe's who was working there as a male nurse came to my bed with an unhappy face. After hesitating for a while, he finally told me that there had been a call-up during the day and that my parents and I were on the list for a transport.

He also explained that I was exempt because of my surgery. I thought it over, but there really was not much to consider. I felt that I belonged with my parents. I had wanted a change, and what on earth would I do all alone in Prague anyway? I remembered how often, during my growing-up years, I had wished to be free of my parents, but suddenly realized how close and dependent we were on each other. I also felt responsible for them, as if they somehow had become my wards over the last few years. The thought of letting them face whatever it was in Terezín alone was more unbearable than the pain in my throat. The next morning, I left the hospital against the advice of the doctor, and before my parents could visit me, I arrived home to help with the packing.

Two days later, we took the tram to the Industrial Palace. An exception was made for our last ride through our beautiful city. We rode along the river, past my childhood playgrounds; past the National Theater and the castle of Hradčany, where for me, despite the fluttering swastika, the ghost of T. G. Masaryk had never left; and the ancient Charles Bridge, where every saint was an old friend of mine. Never before had I realized how much I loved my city. We were all silent during this last passage through Prague. Isolated, yet bound together by our separate memories.

9

I must have fallen asleep, because I remember Mutti shaking me gently and saying that it was time to get up and on line to be counted, that we would march to the train.

At four a.m. we walked through the sleeping streets, five abreast, to the freight yards well out of sight of the rest of the population. Old and young alike were tagged with numbers, written on cards and attached to strings around our necks. Laden like mules with our belongings, we proceeded at a snail's pace, to the great annoyance of the SS escort that walked alongside the columns prodding us and shouting, *Schneller, Schneller, Saujuden, Bewegung.* Incredible confusion at the train. Suitcases had to be put on a separate car, only hand luggage could be kept, and no one was willing to let go of anything. Children were lost, found, and crying, yet in the end this entire human cargo was herded into the waiting train and the doors locked. After more shouting and more delay, the journey began. Terezín was only fifty miles away, but it took until noon to get there.

When the train stopped in Bohušovice, we saw a company of Czech gendarmes standing guard, about two or three dozen SS men guarding the gendarmes and/or us, and a large group of prisoners whose job it was to do the unloading and organizing. Many were friends or relatives of the deportees. One quickly told me to hold on to as much as possible because it was doubtful that we would ever see our larger pieces of luggage again. He also gave me a message that Joe was awaiting me in the ghetto.

The late summer sun was at its zenith, and we were all dressed for Siberia so as to bring along as much warm clothing as we could. Weighed down with backpacks and toting whatever we could possibly carry, we then set out on the longest four-mile hike of my life. Progress was painfully slow, with stragglers being herded over and over again into a semblance of an orderly column. The sun burned down mercilessly on the open road.

People began to stumble and fall, and were picked up by relatives or by the ghetto boys. It was absolute and total misery; nothing mattered but the next step. My post-tonsillectomy throat was a ball of fire, but I was choking with pity for my father, whose neck arteries were visibly throbbing, and my mother, who seemed to get smaller and smaller under her load. Never before or after this moment did I hate those Teutons more. The shouting had stopped and the procession moved in eerie silence. After what seemed an eternity, we reached the ghetto gates.

Terezín was a fortress built under Maria Theresa for a garrison of 3,500 men. During the Republic, an identical number of soldiers were stationed there for military duty, plus about 1,500 civilians, mostly small shopkeepers, innkeepers, and their families. In the summer of 1942, 35,000 Jews were interned there. We were led along the "Main Street" of the ghetto to an outer embankment, into stables with vaulted ceilings and dirty straw spread on the floor. This was to be our quarantine. Quarantine for what? As we walked, I looked for Joe but didn't catch even a glimpse of him. Disappointed and exhausted, I threw myself on the ground and refused to talk or even open my eyes.

Mutti, however, started to scout around for drinking water, tried to coax my father to eat a bite and to nudge me out of my stupor. Ever since the German occupation she had acquired courage and stamina in direct proportion to the adversities that befell us. For as long as I could remember, she had been a pretty fragile creature, given to both real and psychosomatic illnesses. Now she was feeling strong and well, and never even voiced a complaint. Slowly her words started to reach my dulled brain and make sense. Knowing Joe's resourcefulness, she guessed that he had already found a way to meet up with us, and what place would be more likely than the latrine, where everybody had to go?

She was right. When we made our way to that stinkhole, Joe was there, hiding behind a wooden partition. As far as he knew, our transport was in transit; after minor adjustments in its composition, it would leave in forty-eight hours for an unknown destination. But Joe begged us not to worry: we would not be on it since the work he was doing—building the railway spur from Bohušovice station to the ghetto—was considered essential, and families of the railroad workers were protected from further deportations. What he failed to mention, possibly in good faith, was that only his wife was considered immediate family—by no means his in-laws.

Joe also informed us that life in Terezín was quite bearable, if crowded. Once out of quarantine, we would be assigned to permanent quarters and surely adjust to our new environment. Not entirely reassured, we returned to our place in the stables, where we found my father sitting cross-legged on the floor in despair. While we were gone, rumors had been flying, and in no time, everyone learned that Terezín was only the first stop on a much longer trip. New pink call-up slips were distributed, and it was clear that the rumors had been true.

Very few people, like me, received the white slips that signified remaining in Terezín. I tried to assure my parents that there had been some mistake, and that Joe would find a way to fix it, but their optimism was gone. I believe that my father died at this moment, although in reality he lived on for a few more days.

This great gentleman, officer of the Imperial and Royal Austrian Army, this aesthete, was now sitting cross-legged on the floor in a mess of straw. Tears were streaming down his face as he tried to tell me everything that his pride and inhibitions had prevented him from saying for the previous twenty-two years. He told me how his daughter was the center of his universe, how much he loved her, and that he could not possibly go on living without her. Mutti and I were stunned by this totally uncontrollable flood of words. We had each, in our own way, believed that we knew him, but had never witnessed even a faintly similar outburst of feeling. The father I knew only kissed me when he went away on a long trip, and then only on my forehead.

In a burst of defiance, he told us that he would not wait for the Nazis to murder him and my mother. Patting his breast pocket with a strange expression in his face, he confided that he had the means to take care of both of them before things got too difficult: a vial of poison.

I should not have spoken, but I did. I confessed that after we had been arrested in Prague by the Gestapo, I had found the vial in his desk. Suspicious about its contents, I had taken it to a pharmacy to be analyzed and, after discovering what the pills were, had them replaced with saccharine. Then, for the last time, I watched my father fly into one of his familiar rages, shouting that a brat like me had no right to interfere in his affairs.

I felt like a worm. Mutti was as white as a sheet, and it dawned on me that she had known about father's secret escape hatch and now felt as helpless as he. The enormity of what I had done was suddenly clear. Instead of protecting him, I had deprived my father of the last possibility to decide his fate as a free man. I wanted to explain. I wanted to tell them that I had exchanged the pills only because I could not face the idea of being left alone without them. I wanted to tell them how much I loved them, but I could not utter a word.

I went to the Jewish functionaries to protest my exemption and begged them to let me leave with my parents on the transport. They replied that one could not bargain with the *Kommandantur* and, besides, was I perhaps out of my mind? Very little was said during the hours that seemed to drag and slip away at the same time. I hoped against the odds that Joe had been right and that by some miracle two white slips would materialize to save my parents. Another day passed with some shuffling in the composition of the transport and new people arriving to replace the ones who were to stay. With an uncanny certainty that it would be senseless to weigh themselves down with all the bundles scattered around us, Mutti dressed warmly and decided to take only a small bag with some food for the trip. I was to keep everything else with me in Terezín.

With these practicalities taken care of, she calmly told me, *Try to forget what your father said last night. I understand why you did what you did. I probably would also have done it three years ago. You are a grown woman now, and your place is with your husband. Your father and I have had our lives. We have had some wonderful years, and you have given us much joy and pride. Whatever comes now we have to face alone and together. You are very young and your only duty to us is to stay alive. Your life is before you. I know you will be courageous and strong and live to see these evil men punished. God bless you, my little girl.*

The call came to line up for the march back to Bohušovice.

Silently we kissed goodbye, and I walked with them as far as the door of the building when I simply refused to let go of them. I cried and begged to let me go along too, but heard a firm and quiet *No!* from Mutti. The ghetto boys grabbed me from two sides, trying to keep the scene from attracting the attention of the Germans in the yard, and my parents walked away from me, each holding one handle of their little food bag. They never looked back. An excruciating pain shot through my whole body, and I squatted on the floor. I could not stop weeping.

10

When the transport that took my parents left, the rest of us were led into the ghetto and assigned to different barracks. At first, I was quartered in the attic of a huge one called the Hamburger Kaserne, where we were allotted a mattress each. This was placed on top of my two suitcases, which had appeared by some miracle or more likely through the help of Joe's friends.

The drawback of this sleeping arrangement was that anyone over the age of ten wound up with either her head or her feet dragging on the floor. It would have been simpler to sleep directly on the floor, but the mattress provided a way of guarding one's possessions with one's body.

Later that day, the work administrators appeared. Terezín was self-governed, though closely supervised and controlled by the German *Kommandantur*. It had an appointed Jewish Council of Elders and its own hierarchy. Newcomers had to do the hardest and dirtiest jobs for the first one hundred days.

For my first one hundred days, I was assigned as a nurse's aide to a barrack overflowing with old, sick, and demented people. Reporting for work the next evening for the twelve-hour night shift, still weeping and in a state of shock, I found one amateur nurse in charge of a whole floor. She had been in Terezín for more than six months, had adjusted to her dismal surroundings, and had acquired the toughness necessary to keep one's sanity. Capable and extremely busy, she lacked any sympathy for the likes of me.

The barrack was dark but for a few naked bulbs in the long corridors. All the windows were shut and the blinds were drawn due to the blackout. There was no time for an explanation of my duties—just orders shouted on the run: bring water to this patient or take a bedpan to that one. There were about one hundred ghost-like people lying listlessly on their bunks or wandering around in search of food or drink. Two epidemics—dysentery and typhoid fever—were raging. The death rate was high, and the patients who were still alive looked like skeletons. Many had high fevers and were constantly ripping off their clothes and wandering around the corridors stark naked. Every time I looked into one of their faces, it seemed to change into my mother's or father's face. The stench was overpowering, and I didn't know where to run first in response to their cries.

Toward midnight, I became convinced that some were already dead and that their ghosts were trying to drag me down into their abyss. My superior found me vomiting in a corner, remarked sarcastically that this was exactly the sort of help she needed, then turned away in disgust. I knew that she had every right to be annoyed and wished I could sink into the ground and disappear. Somehow, I lived through that night and others like it, but the avalanche of events and emotions were more than I could handle, and I was unable to stop my endless, silent flood of tears.

After a few days in the attic I was assigned permanent sleeping space on the second floor of the Hamburger Kaserne. I came into a large barrack with three tiers of double bunks that held some seventy-two women. There was a Room Elder in command, and I was shown to my place on the middle level of a center bunk. A lovely young face with a halo of snow-white hair appeared smiling on the other side.

She introduced herself as Margot from Breslau, Germany, and said, *I'll help you get comfortable. Things are really not all that bad here. Just wait and see.* We put my stuff away behind the bunk head on a wooden plank, unpacked my blankets and green sheets, while Margot explained that she worked as a seamstress in the children's home and that her husband worked on the railroad siding with Joe. After only five weeks in the ghetto she had worked out a certain routine and seemed, to my amazement, quite happy.

Drawn to Margot's warmth and interest, I told her the miserable story of my last ten days. She did not offer any pious consolation. With what I was to learn was her characteristic tact, Margot just put her arms around me and hugged me tight. I knew then that we would become friends for life.

Evening came and, with it, my other roommates returning from work. My top-bunk neighbor was Mrs. T., one of the most glaring contradictions of the ghetto. The wife of a wealthy jeweler from

Prague, she was a pious convert to Catholicism who never missed her prayers, and seemed to regard herself as a latter-day saint, chosen by God to bear her internment as some sort of stigmata. On the bunk below me lived the sixteen-year-old granddaughter of the Chief Rabbi of Bohemia. Her mother was the Room Elder, and both were lovely, gentle human beings.

Below Margot's bunk was an enormously fat and funny spinster who held court. She came from Frankfurt, Germany, was a born clown, and entertained the whole room with her earthy sense of humor, mostly at her own expense. Above Margot resided Mrs. G., a customer of my mother's who talked incessantly about the furs, clothes, jewels, and other priceless possessions she had abandoned in her exquisite villa in Prague. She was a parvenue par excellence whose studiedly genteel way of speaking vanished when she fought with her oppressed and homely daughter.

After six, the men came to visit. They were allowed to see us until eight, and the room hummed with conversation and laughter. For the first time since my arrival, I was able to look at Joe without hatred when he arrived with Margot's handsome husband, Arthur. The last few days had been hard on my mate. He must have understood that I blamed him for the loss of my parents, even though he had probably saved my life. He tried to console me as well as he could. He pulled out a pack of cigarettes and offered me a few puffs in the hope that this might relax me and stop the flow from my tear ducts.

Smoking was strictly *verboten* in Terezín under penalty of deportation, yet everybody smoked. Cigarettes were the currency of the place. They were smuggled into the ghetto, and for Joe, it was fairly easy because he worked outside and came into daily contact with the Czech laborers working on the railway spur. He had already established regular contact with his Christian friends in Prague through one of them, and was running a busy illegal mail service for himself and his pals who had relatives or sweethearts on the outside.

The largest trade in tobacco was, of course, controlled by the Germans themselves, who sold cigarettes at exorbitant prices and kept these prices up by terror and raids. Everything could be traded for cigarettes, even the skimpy bread rations of some hopelessly addicted smokers. I was to join their ranks very soon.

As we talked to Margot and Arthur and exchanged information and experiences, I realized that Arthur enjoyed none of the advantages that working outside the ghetto entailed. He was a young lawyer from Berlin who had fled to Czechoslovakia, where he and Margot had met at the house of a relative. As Margot told me much later, it was love at first sight. They married and lived on in Prague when their efforts to emigrate came to nothing.

They had learned a smattering of Czech, came to love the city and its people, and had been eventually deported with a Czech transport to Terezín. In his work gang, Arthur was a foreign element, even though he was just as Jewish as the others. His slightly Prussian formality and ignorance of the vernacular put him at a definite disadvantage. Margot, who sewed for others or could charm the cook in the children's home into giving her a few extra portions of food, was better able to augment their rations than Arthur, who had the opportunity but not the savvy.

The young Czech Jews were the elite of the ghetto. There is no doubt that by virtue of their connections with the outside world, they had a much easier time than inmates from Austria, Germany, and, later on, Holland and Denmark. Even if we did not have outside work assignments, the Czech gendarmes who served as our immediate guards were, by and large, sympathetic and helpful to us in establishing communications with the outside world. Many of them had served in the army with our boys. True, they did accumulate a sizable amount of riches in the process, but this does not detract from the very real value of their help.

For Czech Jews, there was always the possibility of working in the kitchen or distribution system, or having a friend or relative working there, since the majority of these posts were manned by native Jews. The older people from other countries who had no family in the ghetto had no such advantage. They were forced to barter away, bit by bit, whatever of their possessions they had managed to salvage for food. There was, for example, a great demand for the plaid lap robes that the German Jews had brought with them in the belief that they were going to Bad Theresienstadt—a spa, the German authorities had led them to believe. This was an indirect bonanza for me. I earned quite a few chunks of salami and bread by fashioning these lap robes into skirts for the more affluent wives and girlfriends of our cooks and quartermasters.

11

The ghetto was, in fact, a microcosm of the society beyond its walls, in all its variety and with all its human traits— good or bad—reinforced. This socioeconomic division was definitely encouraged by the Germans, who endowed certain people with more or less power over the composition of transports, and access to the distribution of food and work. In general, the *Kommandantur* specified only the number of persons, their age, or their national origin in the case of transports. German interference in the day-to-day running of the camp was largely limited to surprise checks and demand for daily reports by the Council of Elders.

My husband had grasped the situation very quickly, adjusted, and made the best of it. Joe was certainly happier here than he had been during his last year in Prague. He felt needed by me and by his friends. The notion that he was able to outsmart the Nazis anytime he wanted gave his damaged ego a tremendous boost. For my twenty-third birthday, the first birthday that I celebrated in captivity—February 26, 1943—Joe produced with great pride a bottle of French perfume and a couple of pork chops that he had smuggled into the camp in hollow shoulder pads.

For me, the period of adjustment to Terezín took a little longer. But after several weeks, I ran into Mrs. W. in the street, and things began to change for the better. Mrs. W. was a former competitor of my mother's who had known me since childhood. After asking me about my parents' whereabouts, she wanted to know what kind of work I was doing in the ghetto.

When I recounted my inept attempts at nursing, she marched me into the Magdeburger Kaserne, where the administrative offices were located. There, she demanded my release from the compulsory hundred-day duty, so that I could work in the workshop she was running for the *Kommandantur*, which produced cheap cotton dresses for the Germans. Out of about one hundred workers there, only a handful were trained dressmakers, and production was limping badly. Later, when she was unable to meet the quota, she was dismissed as forelady and the operation changed into a repair shop for German uniforms. At that moment, though, her arguments carried some weight, partly because they were reasonable but mainly, I suspect, because she happened to be the second or third cousin of somebody in charge of ghetto productions.

This was the way some semblance of normalcy returned to my life. To perform ten hours of work I knew how to do was no hardship. A little rest with friends in the evening helped a good deal, and for the first time in months, I was able to sleep at night. My instinct for self-preservation took over and, with it, the realization that my fate was by no means unique. More important, my interest in other people revived, and I slowly came out of the monumental egotism of an only child.

My marriage had received a severe jolt, never having been on very solid foundations to begin with. Joe and I had never had enough opportunity to get to know each other deeply, and now we had no privacy at all. My feelings about his exploits were ambivalent. I did not like the risks he took, admired but did not share his elation about his successes, yet gladly partook of the advantages they brought. Uneasy about his daily escapades, I never came to a conclusion about why, exactly, he took so many chances, way beyond our immediate need. I envied Margot and Arthur, who were obviously very much in love with each other, and disliked myself for being unable to show my husband even minimal love and appreciation. Other young marriages fell by the wayside because of the insecurity of the future and the wish to squeeze as much pleasure out of life as possible.

The pressures of ghetto life and the constant coming and going of transports made people and relationships quite unpredictable. Old friends very often proved to be impossible to get along with in the suffocating new environment, while strangers became friends for life. A whole new standard of behavior evolved, much of it self-sacrificing and noble, but also frequently selfish and amoral. Religion began to fascinate me for a second time in my life. As a child I had been totally captivated by the mysticism of the Catholic ritual; now I was suspicious of Mrs. T. and other converts who were able to keep their faith intact in spite of the absurdity of the situation.

My friend (and Joe's first cousin) Vava was nominally a Catholic since birth. Her parents, like my own, were agnostics. She was now coming full circle back to Judaism under the influence of a Viennese rabbi who was a friend of hers. I did not quite relate to either Judaism or Catholicism. Out of a sense of isolation, I had gone to a midnight mass the first Christmas in camp that had been celebrated secretly in one of the many attics. Some fifty people of all ages had been present, going through the familiar motions. It was eerie. Not having the foundation of a true believer, I felt nothing: no consolation, no presence of God.

Later, I accompanied Vava to a Sabbath service in the oldest and most dismal barrack of Terezín. Here I found old men in prayer shawls, swaying and lost in a world I could not enter or even begin to comprehend. I left puzzled. Vava said that I was supposed to feel a kinship with these people, but I felt like a stranger and was absolutely unmoved. I wanted to do something more tangible to give some reason to our existence than to pray to a God who so obviously had forsaken us. I was, however, equally turned off by the very active but secret Zionist and Communist groups in Terezín.

A movement had sprung up at this time, where young couples like Joe and I, who were relatively better off than the rest of the prisoners, unofficially adopted children who were alone in Terezín because their parents were dead or imprisoned in different camps. The idea was to give them a small substitute for their families and also to improve their health by sharing the small surplus of food we had.

The official food rations were minimal. A typical daily allotment consisted of a three-inch piece of dark bread, two cups of black coffee—the resemblance to real coffee was purely accidental—a portion of pea or lentil soup (about a dozen dots swimming in the dark water), three or four potatoes boiled in their skin, and one ladle of tomato or mustard sauce or perhaps a piece of turnip. Meat was doled out sparsely and called goulash: this was brown gravy with a few cubes of horsemeat. Only meat stamped by the department of food supplies as "unfit for human consumption" was used. An extra bonus could be the occasional one-inch slice of salami, a third of a small can of liver spread, a one-inch square of margarine, or a tablespoon of prune butter. The children received somewhat better fare, mainly because it was cooked separately, but their diet was by no means conducive to their growth.

Joe and I went to the children's house to select a child to adopt. There was quite a choice available, and the lady in charge thought that in view of my own young age, we would all be best off with a three- to five-year-old. While we were discussing the matter, I noticed a dark-haired girl of about nine with enormous brown eyes standing alone in a corner, watching. Against the misgivings of the counselor, I insisted on adopting Gisa, who turned out to be twelve and did not say one word about our proposed arrangement, but consented to go for a walk to get acquainted with us. According to her file, Gisa's parents had been taken away at the time of the annexation of the Sudetenland and not been heard of again. She and her older brother were placed in an orphanage in Karlsbad and, after the occupation, transferred to another one in Prague. Four years later the whole institution was evacuated to Terezín.

Gisa's brother was already sixteen and had to work. He lived in the men's barracks and did not see her too often. Like a little mouse, she was suspicious of everything and everybody, and it took me weeks to coax a smile from her. In spite of obviously being hungry most of the time, she only nibbled at whatever we offered her and put part of it carefully in her pocket to eat later or maybe share with her brother—I never found out. When we gave her a piece of chocolate, we discovered that she had never seen or tasted chocolate before.

Gisa finally melted one day when I threw a few English words into our conversation with Joe. *You speak* English! she cried out. *Will you teach me?* From then on, we were friends. I taught her one hour a day, improvising as we went along. She soaked it up like a sponge and also happily started to eat more and fill out a little. I made over some of my clothes for her, because the outgrown things she was wearing made her look even tinier than she actually was. She became somewhat more communicative and even displayed a certain degree of vanity one day after she saw her reflection in a window on the street.

She talked about her parents, and as time went by, she told me more and more of what she remembered from the time when they were still with her. She never cried and always retained a certain very grown-up distance. She evidently accepted me as a friend, but there was no fantasy that I could possibly replace her mother.

12

During 1943, my own life seemed relatively stable even though transports were incessantly coming and going. Outgoing transports always created panic, and endless finagling over who was to go and who to stay. Sometimes it was only young people capable of work; other times, only the old and sick. The railroad spur from Bohušovice was still far from complete, and Joe and I did not worry too much. Rumors ran wild: this was to be the last transport, or the war was about to be over tomorrow, next week, at the latest in three months.

Small wonder that in this kind of atmosphere Margot and I decided to see a palm reader. We had heard about the old lady from Germany and visited her one evening in one of the barracks for the aged. We sat with her by the window. I studied her still-beautiful face while she held my hand between her wrinkled fingers. After a long pause she looked me in the face and said, *Child, you have a young and handsome husband, but I see you as a widow. He is engaged*

in something that will cost him his life. You will live and marry a man
you have known since your childhood. You will leave Europe and go
with him over the great ocean to raise a new family.

I wanted to know what had happened to my parents, but she
would not tell me and turned to Margot. She shook her head and
said, *Too many widows, too many widows,* and after telling Margot
some astonishing true events from her past, the palm reader assured her that she, too, would live but that her husband would not.
We left a little unsettled and tried very hard to ridicule the whole
episode, but it was difficult to forget her words.

In spite of all this, life could be pleasant, even amusing at times.
There was chamber music, singing to the accompaniment of an
accordion; opera; drama; and poetry readings produced under unbelievably difficult conditions. Scenery was created with stolen
planks from the lumberyard, where many prisoners worked, and
out of rags and empty potato sacks. Scores were copied by hand
and music written down from memory and new works composed.
Never again have I heard a more moving performance of the Verdi
Requiem. Especially the "Libera Me" took on added significance
when sung in Terezín by a brilliant young soprano from Berlin.
Three weeks later she was deported "to the East."

The amount of talent assembled in this godforsaken place was
utterly astonishing and impossible to keep shackled. Artists were
painting, drawing, and writing on every scrap of paper they could
lay hands on. And there were discussions, debates, and endless
talking. Whenever an outgoing transport disrupted an art project,
more artists appeared to take the place of the ones who had to go.

But the talent barrel was not bottomless, and by the end of the war only a pitiful remnant survived.

There were soccer games every Saturday afternoon, weather permitting. They were played in the courtyard of the Dresdner Kaserne, which had wide-open, loggia-like corridors all around. The perfect setting for a bullfight and almost as many people present. Everyone dressed in their best and cheered his team at the top of their lungs. For a few hours we were oblivious to the reality of the camp.

The older women, the mothers and grandmothers, were the most amazing inhabitants of our anthill. They had by far more energy and resourcefulness than their mates and managed, after a full day's work, to transform the few potatoes of our daily rations into tasty concoctions and their bunks into minuscule homes. Complaints were rarely heard, and their good manners prevailed even in unavoidable disputes, when they would hurl accusations or reproaches at each other, always addressing one another by the titles of their respective husbands. Their only indulgence was the fond recall of things left behind, and these former possessions seemed to grow as time went by until one would believe that there had been only rich Jews in our former life. I found this harmless, amusing, and seldom malicious.

After working for some time on damaged uniforms, I was combing my hair one day when I noticed little creatures crawling on the comb. For a moment I was too stunned to move, and then I burst into my dorm screaming that I had lice, *LICE*, and that I would never, never get rid of them and that Margot must have them too because we shared one bunk.

She was much less excitable than I and noted that I was not the first to be loused up. She "organized" (stole) a large can of kerosene from somewhere, and we doused our hair with kerosene for the next three days until we both developed eczema. The next problem was to get the stuff out of our hair with only cold water available, but we managed and turned our attention back to our regular nightly flea hunt. Our system was to light a candle with the blankets over our heads. A fire risk? Yes, but we developed an expertise in tracking down our tormentors.

Soon after this I came down with the mumps. Not just a normal case but, probably due to all the rinsing with cold water, a monumental one. I grew into the shape of an oversized pear, with only my forehead retaining its normal size, to the great amusement of my room and the doctor, who brought around his colleagues to show off this rarity of a patient. Needless to say, I did not find the situation funny at all, and when even Joe and Margot could not suppress their laughter at the sight of me, I got really furious. Children's diseases were rampant in the ghetto, and anyone who missed them as a child was sure to catch up now.

When I first arrived in Terezín, I had not been able to see my childhood best friend, Kitty, because she was quarantined with scarlet fever. This was a great disappointment for us both. Kitty and I had been inseparable since childhood: she was my second cousin and my alter ego since her birth two years after I was born. Living on the same block and both being only children, we had practically grown up together. Kitty had arrived in Terezín in December 1941 with one of the first transports, and we had missed each other badly during the eight months that we were separated. Her parents were in the ghetto as well. Her father was a House Elder and protected from further transports by virtue of being a prominent member of the community. She had come out of the hospital happy as a lark to see me, full of funny stories about doctors and nurses.

Kitty had a Terezín boyfriend by the name of Bubi, who became fast friends with Joe. The fact that she had a Christian fiancé back in Prague did not bother her too much for the moment. Things could always be explained later when the time came. Like many of the Czech old-timers, she was living in relative comfort with three other girls in a small room off the corridor in my barracks.

With characteristic generosity and a twinkle in her eye, she immediately offered Joe and me the use of her room for a few hours as a love nest. The four girls had worked out an elaborate schedule to accommodate their three love affairs and one marriage. In the evenings I used to visit them, and the entertainment there was always superb. Aside from the high spirits of this foursome, we very often enjoyed the visit of one of their beaus, a professional nightclub musician, who was a wizard in sneaking into the women's barrack after curfew. With his accordion the music and singing lasted often long into the night.

Kitty's boyfriend, Bubi, was in the ghetto police. This was a rather operetta-like outfit that was supposed to keep order, but very often helped along with all kinds of shenanigans to fool the gendarmes or the Nazis, at least the ones with a sense of humor.

The following year Bubi, Joe, and another ghetto watchman

named Honza built a *kumbal*. This was a roofless shed put up in several attics of the former residential houses in Terezín. It measured about nine feet by fifteen feet, and was made of "organized lumber" paid for with cigarettes and other contraband. Furnished with three cots and a few shelves, and decorated with our beautiful green sheets, the place had the look of a miniature weekend cottage and afforded a little bit of rare privacy, particularly since all the boys were working different shifts.

In any event there were never any quarrels about when it was desirable for two of the residents to disappear for a while. What was really nice about it was that we now had a corner of our own where we could see our friends on a Sunday afternoon—have a cup of real coffee without the prying glances of a dorm full of people, some conversation, and the illusion that everything was quite normal.

Of course it was just that—an illusion—because transports never stopped, friends were gone from one day to the other, and the death rate of the older generation soared. I will never forget the old-fashioned hearses drawn by people, moved up and down the streets alternately carrying corpses out of the ghetto and half-rotten potatoes in, and how their peculiar combination of odors hung in the air.

I lived under the administration of three Jewish Elders. The first was Jakob Edelstein, a Zionist of Polish origin, very capable and unafraid to stand his ground before the *Kommandantur*. He was replaced by Paul Eppstein from Berlin, who was by far less courageous, and had a tendency to favor his countrymen. He trembled before the Germans and often kowtowed beyond the call of necessity. The third was Benjamin Murmelstein, a Viennese rabbi.

These men and the Council of Elders had power and privilege, but their situation was not simple and they had no choice in the matter. What they *did* have was better and more food, better housing, the privilege of living with their wives, and the power to assign work and decide who left Terezín and when. So long as these men—and they were only human—were influenced only by their convictions as to who was worth saving, there could be no reasonable quarrel with their decisions. But when they were guided by considerations for friends and friends of friends and third and fourth cousins or in some cases by outright bribery, it became a radically different picture.

This system extended like a staircase down through the lower levels of ghetto administration and was part of a clever plan to set one prisoner against the other. The *Cripo*, or Jewish criminal plainclothes police, was based on spying and denouncing fellow inmates. It was not always successful but in too many instances played right into the hands of some power-drunk or sadistic person. Jews are no different from other people. The longer I lived in Terezín, the more I learned how difficult it was to preserve a value system, assuming that a person was mature enough to have one.

13

On December 15 and 18 of 1943, two transports with a total of 5,007 young people left Terezín. The reason, we were told, was that because of overcrowding in the ghetto, these people were needed to build a new one elsewhere. I am quite sure that the Council of Elders knew more about their destination than they let us know, but kept quiet, fearing for their own skins in the event of mass escapes or a possible uprising.

The events of November 11 were still fresh in everyone's memory. That day, the entire population of the ghetto—about forty-five thousand people—was marched out into a deserted field. We stood there all day in the drizzling rain, surrounded by Czech gendarmes with submachine guns, being counted and recounted by the SS. Shivering and frightened, many of us were convinced that we would never make it back to the ghetto alive. The census was inconclusive—there were people missing—and by midnight, we were marched back to our barracks, hungry and exhausted.

After this happened, Joe and I expected to leave with the December transports. The railway spur to Bohušovice was nearly complete, and Joe became very concerned about the elimination of the reason for his deferment from transports. To be on the safe side, he hit upon the brilliant idea that if I could possibly come down with scarlet fever, we would be covered on two fronts.

Our good friend Dr. V. gave me a strong shot of the bacteria, offering it first to Joe, who claimed to be immune because he had come down with the disease as a child. Then we waited for the symptoms to appear. Fortunately, I never got more than a headache and a slight temperature—no spots, not enough to be quarantined. No spots, no quarantine was the rule, and we were not called up after all.

Kitty was not that lucky. She had turned twenty-one the month before and was no longer entitled to be listed on the "protected" list with her parents. Her boyfriend, Bubi, and Joe's roommate, Honza, were deported at the same time, as were the majority of our friends. We all parted in a rather lighthearted way. Kitty even promised to keep the bunk next to her warm for me. Stupidly, we believed the story about a new ghetto.

A lull followed the departure of this group. Transports stopped going out. They only came in: now the Dutch and the Danes. But, in fact, great changes were taking place. The outer fortress, which had served as quarantine hall when I arrived, was not used for that purpose anymore, but was made into a gigantic warehouse for articles that had been confiscated over the past years. My uniform workshop was closed, and I was transferred to this warehouse, to sort and repair clothes so that the best could be shipped to the Reich.

Much stranger things were going on. The houses on the main street were being painted on the outside. Shops that had been converted into dorms were now being reconverted into stores, with display windows that displayed some of the best pieces we could find in the warehouse. More for display than for sale. A café was opened, with music, where one could visit for one hour with special coupons. Money was printed and a bank opened. An enormous circus tent that had been put up the year before to house mica production was hurriedly torn down and a music pavilion built on the town square. The ground was reseeded with grass; benches and even a playground were built.

In January, the Hamburger Kaserne that housed 3,500 women was completely evacuated. The barrack was converted into a processing station at the end of the now-finished railroad spur. In the ensuing confusion of reassigning spaces, I moved in with Joe, who was now alone in his *kumbal*.

On January 20, a passenger train filled with well-dressed people pulled in, and the reason for all the mysterious changes became clear. The newly arrived guests were Dutch Jews who were greeted personally by the Council of Elders with welcoming speeches. The SS *Kommandant* in person and his henchmen helped women and children from the cars, and the whole elaborate production was filmed for newsreels, later to be shown all over Europe as proof of how well Jews were traveling under the protection of the German Reich. Right after the welcome, these people were given postcards to write to their friends in Holland, to assure them of their well-being. Better was yet to come. The name Ghetto Terezín was changed to the Jewish Settlement Theresienstadt, and inmates did not have to salute the SS anymore, or stand at attention, or step off the sidewalk when passing them.

Failure to do those things had previously brought a lashing of ten strokes. The apartments of the prominent members of the Council of Elders were redecorated and furnished with Danish modern furniture. Obviously something more important than a newsreel was up.

14

Since the railroad spur was now finished, only a limited number of workers were retained for maintenance. After a mad scramble for these few remaining places, Joe managed to hold on, but his trips to Bohušovice now occurred at irregular intervals, when some work on the circular saw was needed. Contacts with his Christian counterparts became more complicated and visible.

One night during this time I had a dream. In it, I found myself in a place I had never seen before. It was like a forest of barbed wire where the ground had an unusual ocher color I had not seen anywhere in Central Europe. There were flashes of light shooting through a dark purple sky. I was all alone but had the feeling of thousands of eyes watching me. I awoke by my own screams, surprised to find myself in my bunk with Joe staring at me. Neither he nor Margot or any other of our friends had ever seen a place like this, and after much discussion, the nightmare remained a puzzle.

Then, one evening early in March, Joe told me that he was

worried about an incident that had happened that day. He was sup-posed to meet his contact in Bohušovice, but could not go because, at the last minute, another maintenance man was sent out. In order not to hold up communications, Joe had asked the man to take a note and money to his contact but, in case he missed him, not to bring it back into the ghetto. In that case, the man should leave the wad of paper in a pile of railroad ties stacked near the saw.

In the evening, Joe discovered to his horror that the two men had not only missed each other, but that the man had brought the little wad back and, trying to hide it overnight, had stuffed it into the hollow roll of a blackout shade. One of the few rats among the Czech gendarmes was standing across the dark street watching him do this and made a report to the *Kommandantur*. A few min-utes later, the SS came into the dorm, went to the window, threat-ened the occupants of the whole room with reprisals, and took away their man. The note was signed only *Joe from the hut*, but it was very doubtful that this man would hold out for very long with-out giving Joe's full name.

There was nothing to do but to report for work the next morn-ing as usual, but after a few hours, a friend of ours who worked at the gendarmerie as an orderly came to fetch me with the news that Joe was being arrested. A gendarme had already left to bring him to the *Kommandantur*. I would be able to see Joe—as if by coincidence—on his way through the ghetto, but the situation ap-peared bleak. I ran to the gate to meet them and saw Joe coming down the road, handcuffed to the gendarme. Suddenly, I remem-bered the palm reader and trembled with fear. Joe had aged ten years since the day before. All the color was drained from his face, and his first words to me were that everything was lost.

I tried to give him courage and mainly begged him not to involve his Christian friend, since they did not know his name. Joe replied that he was scared and that he did not believe he had the strength to withstand interrogation should he be tortured. Later, I discovered that this was exactly what happened and that, aside from his contact, he had dragged in one more person. A few days later he was sent to the "Small Fortress," the high-security prison near Terezín.

The tensions of the last years had finally taken their toll. I felt great pity for Joe but, at the same time, was angry at him. I also felt terribly guilty toward the wives of the other ten men who were now compromised because of their association with my husband.

Our friends rallied around me, trying to keep up my morale. My friend, Joe's cousin Vava, got busy trying to get me on the "protected" list of someone high on the Council of Elders. She achieved this in a very roundabout way without my personally doing a thing, or even meeting the gentleman in question. She was a good friend of the rabbi who was the head of the Council of Elders at the time. Through her good offices, I became part of his official household.

Unable to keep the *kumbal* to myself, I was assigned two new roommates. One was the girlfriend of a young pianist and composer, Gideon Klein. I was once again in a strange and restless mood, almost destructive of whatever security I had left, both wishing for and fearing some sort of change. For the moment, in view of the beautification program, there was little harassment, but incoming transports changed the national composition and made the ghetto population rise again.

My friends visited me every day. Particularly Dr. V. and F. O.—great pals and former clients of Joe's—checked to see whether I had enough to eat and to guard me against the wolves. It took me a while to discover that they were actually watching one another because, both having Christian fiancées in Prague, each suspected the other of having improper designs on me. Fooling around with the wife of a jailed friend was considered—even by ghetto standards—taboo. No one evidently credited me with enough judgment to look after myself.

Gideon Klein was staging and directing a production of *Carmen* at the time, with the blessing and even the help of the *Kommandant*, who made the use of their gym building available for the production. I went to a few rehearsals with his girlfriend, and these were experiences not easy to forget. Mounting an opera production with all the obstacles of ghetto life was nothing short of a miracle.

Sometime earlier, another interesting man had become part of our immediate circle. He was a well-known Czech writer, who was allotted a *kumbal* in our building and by special permission allowed to live with his companion of many years. Not only did he receive all his luggage, but also a whole bookcase of books. He gave me the run of them, and I started to read most of Dostoyevsky. The volume that made the deepest impression on me was *Notes from a Dead House*, a relatively short work about the prison camps of Siberia. I did not miss the analogies to our situation, and we had long discussions about who learned what from whom.

I had another protector at work. A Czech gendarme named Karel, brother of the gendarme who had to arrest Joe. Karel had also known Joe for a long time as a friend and helper. Karel now made it his business to look after me, namely to feed me whenever he was on duty. He used to come into my place of work, gruffly call me out, and take me to the guardroom, where he locked me in with a package of sandwiches and pickles his mother had prepared. Fifteen minutes later, he led me back with a loud admonition to work harder.

One day, he brought me a little crumpled note from Joe that said only that he was well and that he loved me. Karel told me that Joe was working on the truck that brought coal to the fortress and that if I was lucky I could see him someday because a little stretch of the road was visible from the window of the guardroom. I saw many trucks pass by, but they passed so quickly that I was never sure whether I had seen Joe or not. Just in case, I waved to all of them.

Spring brought persistent rumors about a visit by an International Red Cross commission. *Kommandant* Burger was replaced by the Austrian Rahm, who showed more understanding for the project of presenting to the commission a showpiece of humanitarian concern. The children in the orphanage were drilled to answer *Chocolate again, Uncle Rahm!* in case the *Kommandant* visited the children's home with the commission.

The success of this indoctrination was highly doubtful, and one infamous place of the ghetto certainly defied the sprucing-up operation completely. This was the mental ward. No amount of paint or white sheets could change the devastation in the faces of the inmates.

This made the Nazis quite uneasy, as well as the fact that the population had once again topped 40,000. To solve the problem, they planned three transports of 2,500 people each, leaving in intervals of two days, beginning May 15. Included were the orphanage and the mental ward, and a cross-section of the population with many young people who were considered potential troublemakers.

I was called up too. My remaining friends tried to pull every available string but soon discovered that my deportation had been ordered by name from the *Kommandantur*, as a reprisal against Joe's infraction of the ghetto rules. There were three others in the same situation: two wives of the other men involved in the affair and the four-year-old son of one of the couples.

Dr. Murmelstein tried until the last minute to save us, but with the third batch on May 18, we had to show up at the Hamburger Kaserne, all packed, tagged, and ready to go. We were hidden in a room facing out onto the waiting train while the Council of Elders delivered the requisitioned 2,500 people. We hoped that with the quota filled, the SS might mercifully forget us, and watched the loading of the train the whole day, one cattle car after another being filled, locked, and sealed. At five forty-five p.m. the last car was filled.

We held our breaths, hoping that the train would now move, when we heard a big commotion in the corridor and an unmistakable voice shouting. The door burst open.

Who are these people?

These are the special orders, Kommandant, replied Dr. Murmel-stein. *Only women and a child.*

What are you trying to do, put something over on me? Raus! Raus! Into the train, but fast! Saujuden.

They opened the last car and we were literally thrown in, our bundles after us. The door slammed shut and the train left with 2,504 people.

15

nside it was dark, and it took quite a while to discern any figures. The car was so full that we could sit only with our legs pulled up to our bodies. It also happened to be the car containing the inmates of an old-age barrack, most of whom were sick and shocked out of their wits.

Our little group crouched near the door where we had landed, quietly sobbing. Terezín had been no paradise, but right now, it seemed so. I suppose I even felt worse than the rest, because I held myself indirectly responsible for their being on the transport. I felt bitterly sorry for all of us, but mostly for the little one huddled in his mother's arms.

These were my last actual tears, though I was to cry for the duration of the war. There was a barred window at each end of the car and two pails in a corner. One was meant to serve as a toilet; the other contained water. Both of them were too small for the eighty-odd people crammed together. After a few hours, we tried to bring a little order into the chaos around us.

At dawn the train stopped for a while. The door opened a foot and one pail was emptied on the tracks, while the guards refilled the other with water. As the trip continued, there were two more stops, but the stench, thirst, and moaning became almost unbearable. I thought of my parents. They had been in this same situation. But then I remembered someone from the *Transportleitung* telling me, at the time, that they had left on a passenger train, even occupying window seats. That relaxed me somewhat, and I resigned myself to whatever would come.

It was late the next night when we stopped at a platform with a big sign that read AUSCHWITZ. At this point, the name did not have any meaning for me. I only realized that we were in Poland because the other half of the sign read OŚWIĘCIM. Even before the doors opened, I heard a lot of bellowing in German and Polish. The cursing became louder when the cars were opened, and I saw on the ramp, aside from what seemed to be a whole detachment of SS men, a large number of strange creatures in striped blue-and-gray pajamas with shaved heads making almost as much noise as the Germans.

We were chased out of the car at breakneck speed, with only our clothes and the contents of our pockets. Our bundles left behind, we were pushed and jostled into a long column and made to march a dirt road. It was flanked on both sides by double walls of barbed wire, marked at intervals with little signs reading ACHTUNG HOCHSPANNUNG ("Caution: High Voltage," in German). The whole spooky scene was illuminated by beacon-like light beams emanating from watchtowers every few hundred yards. There were dark structures visible behind the wires and dogs and SS men everywhere.

A few striped figures flitted back and forth in the dark, carefully keeping out of the way of the SS. About halfway through this trek, one of these creatures materialized next to me at one end of a stretcher with a covered corpse and said, *Nazdar!* ("Hi," in Czech). Startled, I recognized our friend Tommy, who had left Terezín in December. He looked old and hungry and explained hurriedly that everything of value would be taken from us, that Joe's old roommate Honza had sent him with the message to give him whatever I wanted to save and he would smuggle it into camp. I had very little: two wristwatches, a fountain pen, a toothbrush, a comb, some stockings. Pushing this under the cloth with the corpse, Tommy disappeared in the dark without being noticed.

We were brought to a large, stable-like barrack, separated from the men, and made to form single lines in front of tables where female Polish prisoners in striped uniforms were registering our data. The SS left and soon Honza himself came in and led me to the back of the room. He told me that the registration process would take hours, and I might as well sit down and eat something. He explained that we were in Birkenau, that it was part of the Auschwitz concentration camp. Here, in the so-called "Family Camp," Czech men and women were held in the same compound.

He told me that I was now in quarantine for processing. That meant registration, tattooing, work assignment, body search, and general intimidation. The rest of the prisoners were forbidden to have any contact with us for the duration; Honza was only able to be present because he happened to be the Block Elder—or *Capo*, as they were called here—of this barrack, which normally was the children's house. It was the only place that received somewhat better food, and that was why he was able to feed me. He had already heard about Joe's arrest from the boys in the previous transport and had, in fact, been expecting me.

Honza now became my guardian angel. He had sent Tommy and offered to keep my watches for an emergency, in case I should get sick and need drugs. He considered the children's house one of the safest places in camp—which it was, for reasons I could never quite put my finger on. His deputy was the husband of a former apprentice of my mother's. He looked me over after joining us and remarked offhandedly that I would never be able to keep the riding boots I was wearing and offered to salvage them for me.

I missed a signal from Honza's eyes and agreed. His feet were small for a man, but the swap was made. My boots obviously pinched his feet while I slid around in his shoes, yet he was terribly happy about the deal and I really did not care at this point. Besides, he promised we would swap again when the heat was off.

During this first long night, I also learned to beware of the Polish prisoners, who hated the Jews just as much as the Nazis did and often more. All prisoners had to wear little colored triangles on their sleeves to denote their status, such as Jews, Political, or Criminal. Some of these categories overlapped: for example, there were Jews among those who were classified Political. Generally, they were Communists, Socialists, or adherents of a variety of opposition groups from all over Europe. Some of them had been imprisoned from five to eight years before coming to Auschwitz.

There was no doubt that the Poles were the most powerful of all, mainly because they had been in Auschwitz right from its inception in 1941. Due to their natural tendency to anti-Semitism, they had the ears of the Germans in many instances and made the most of it. Most of these people had been arrested individually for specific or preventive reasons.

The Criminal contingent was exactly what the word means: no different from criminals elsewhere, with many of them serving life sentences. By virtue of their long tenure, many were *Capos* and scribes in various other sections of the concentration camp and consequently had access to more information than only Birkenau. Typically, a good many became rather friendly with some SS men— maybe a case of kinship of souls? At the bottom of the scale were the Jews and gypsies. We were not considered political prisoners, although to my thinking, we were just that.

The lines at the tables were slowly thinning. My lesson was ended. Honza needed some sleep, and I got up to await my turn. The scribes were tired out, and less hostile and bossy than in the beginning. After giving my personal data, I quickly and painlessly acquired a tattoo on my left forearm. I was assigned to Block 12, with most of the old women who had fallen back to the end of the lines. This dismayed me a little but turned into a stroke of luck.

The *Capo* of Block 12 happened to be a friend from Terezín, where she had been a cook and I had made a few clothes for her. She now welcomed me with open arms and favored me from the start. She assigned me a choice upper bunk near a little window, slipped me a piece of bread or salami once in a while, and also made sure that I got my soup from the bottom of the barrel. Nina* was a leftover from the September 1943 transport, with a fairly solid position in camp, largely because she was exquisitely beautiful, with blue eyes and long blond hair, and because a criminal German *Capo* was deeply and sincerely in love with her. This way she was not only able to keep her mother with her and eat better, but our block also received less harassment than the others.

At dawn, a strange little man sporting an armband with the initials *CP* (Criminal Police) appeared and started pacing up and down the long brick horizontal chimney that ran down the length of the barrack. He was a Jew like the rest of us, but endowed with a highly exaggerated sense of his own importance: a perfect caricature of an SS man—except that he was not trying to be funny. He had become just like his masters.

He gave a very strict lecture on the dos and don'ts of the camp, threatening fire and brimstone. He made it perfectly clear that we were not allowed to keep *anything*. Coats longer than twenty inches? *Verboten*. Also extra stockings, jewelry, shoes, and, naturally, money. He warned that we would be searched and searched again and that noncompliance would carry severe penalties.

If I had not been so stunned and tired, I would have laughed at this extraordinary performance. As it was, I got busy as soon as he left. I took out of my pocket the little nail scissors I still had and began to cut to size my still-beautiful camel-hair coat. It was the

---

* Editor's note: Names that I am certain are pseudonyms are marked with asterisks.

last remnant of our spring collection of 1939, a copy of a Marcel
Roche. It took hours to cut through the heavy material and longer
to hem it, using the threads I pulled out of the seams.

Just as I finished, our *Cripo*-Clown returned with a few helpers
and a search began. Coats piled up on the chimney. Rings, fountain pens, lipsticks, even buttons were collected in a bag. When
they came up to me, I just shrugged.

You still have your wedding ring! the *Cripo* snarled. *Who do you
think you are? Some sort of privileged character?*

In the heat of salvaging my coat, I had forgotten the ring. Now
I slowly pulled it off and threw it in his bag.

16

Kitty came running into the barrack as soon as quarantine was lifted.

Why did you come here? You fool, don't you know that we're all going to be burned June twentieth? You should have run away after they locked up Joe. The only reason why we from December are still alive is that the bastards want a nice round number for the operation and there weren't enough of us left from March. Don't you know that to commemorate Masaryk's birthday, they sent 3,750 young people up the chimney? The March transport was brought in to replace them. Nobody leaves here alive. The limit is six months and no more. Why on earth did you have to come?

I sat there, convinced that she had gone raving mad. This could not possibly be my lifelong pal, the social butterfly with beautiful dark eyes that always smiled, even when she was serious. Now they could not hold still even for a moment. They shifted back and forth while she blurted out this totally irrational nonsense. Why hadn't Honza said one word about all this?

A very strange sensation took hold of me then. I stared down at my tattooed arm, and like a badly focused picture in a camera, it slowly detached itself and became two arms. But only one had a tattoo. I tried to focus back, but the movement continued until there were two of us: me and A-4116. I thought, *What is she doing here, poor devil? I know her. I'm sorry for her. I'll watch her. She looks just like me.*

Listen to me, said Kitty. *I can see by your face that you don't believe one word I said. Come out and I'll show you.*

A-4116 climbed down from her bunk and followed Kitty out into the camp. There, in the distance, Kitty showed her a group of chimneys spewing smoke into the sky, and for the first time since her arrival, she became conscious of a peculiar odor in the air, like burning hair or bones.

Still incredulous, A-4116 said, *But all this is quite impossible. Anyway, how do you know? This is a big camp and they might just be burning corpses of people who died a natural death. You know how Germans are about cleanliness. Besides, there're enough old and sick people around to keep a crematorium busy.*

Oh yeah? said Kitty. *Then how do you explain that 3,750 people disappeared overnight?*

They could have been deported somewhere else. This is 1944. There are international laws. They could never get away with murder on a scale like this. Have you forgotten that there is still a world out there that could do the same thing to German prisoners?

Shit, you are so naive. The world doesn't give a hoot what happens to us here—for all we know, they might not even believe it if they saw it. Just like you. What about your Capo, Nina. Why do you think she stayed alive—and with her mother at that? That boyfriend of hers went through all kinds of trouble to stash them both away on the typhus quarantine block because HE knew what was up and he also knew that the typhus block would not be taken. They are all here in your own block. Go ask her.

The two girls were walking up and down the camp road as they talked, stopping here and there to greet old friends. A-4116 noticed how much everybody seemed changed in the months since she had seen them in Terezín. They were all thinner, and their clothes and shoes made them look like extras out of *The Beggar's Opera*. Everybody seemed to be clutching a little bundle and be in a hurry to get somewhere. Since this was the only time of the day when men and women were allowed to see each other, the road was very crowded.

There were seven barracks on each side of the road, with the latrine in the center of the women's row. Birkenau formed a quadrangle surrounded by two rows of loaded high-voltage barbed wire. At one end was a large gate dominated by a large sign reading ARBEIT MACHT FREI ("Work Makes You Free"). Beyond the gate were the guardhouses of the SS. At the other end one could see a railway yard. On both sides, the same kind of gigantic cages stretched as far as the eye could see.

Appell sounded and everybody had to return to their barracks. This was a twice-daily routine and lasted from one to three hours, depending on how quickly the officer in charge could add. The inhabitants of every barrack had to stand outside in perfect rows of five and come to attention when the SS officer arrived. The *Capo* reported the number present, sick, or dead. The SS entered the barrack to check on the accuracy and recounted the assembled prisoners. A-4116 watched the proceedings with detached interest, amused at the frantic efforts of the *Capo* and her two helpers, a deputy and a scribe, to keep the rows straight and neat—a difficult task, since they were dealing with people not drilled in military discipline.

Her amusement faded when it was explained in whispers that if the rows were not perfect, blows would fall on the *Capo*'s head and the whole camp would be made to stand until order was established. The *Capo* across the road in the men's Block 13 was so zealous that he boxed and slapped his men into shape even before the officer arrived.

She recognized him. It was Richard, who had been part of her crowd in Terezín. What had happened to him? She knew he was a tough sort of guy who played center forward on the soccer team and was not very choosy about the expressions he used. But what he displayed now was out-of-control brutality. She wondered whether his attitude had also changed toward the girl he had a relationship with in Terezín, whom she knew quite well.

Appell over, it was chow time. Soup and a bread ration about three inches thick, to last for the next twenty-four hours. Some people would eat it in one sitting; others would carefully divide it up into three pieces, eat one, and hide the rest in a little bundle under their straw mattress. It was getting dark quickly now. The lights were turned out. The day was over.

A-4116 lay on her bunk, her eyes wide open, unable to fall asleep despite not having slept for the last sixty hours. Images were chasing each other as in a crazy film montage. Chimneys, raggedy people, Kitty's eyes, chimneys, Honza with his gentle smile, chimneys, Richard hitting and bellowing at some old man, barbed wire, German shepherds, chimneys, Nina, Mutti's face, Father—where were they?—until it all became a fiery ball spinning before her eyes. Faintly, she seemed to hear Mutti's voice: *Your only duty to us is to stay alive.*

I will, she said out loud. *I will*.

17

Unsurprisingly, A-4116 was assigned to the sewing shop. Judging by the uniforms that came in for repair, the war was not going too well for the Germans. In Terezín, there had been torn-off buttons and ripped linings; in Birkenau, there were gaping holes that had to be patched and dark stains that could only have been blood. Still, the uniforms had to be repaired for further use.

This was small consolation for an empty stomach. In the evening, she sometimes went for a walk with Kitty to see Honza at the children's block, where Gisa also lived. The children all worshipped him, instinctively sensing his inherent goodness. His mother worshipped him too, and this was a decidedly two-way affair, since his father had died when he was a young boy. Here, as in Terezín, they always walked arm in arm, and no girl ever got close to tying Honza down, although he was one of the most attractive and eligible bachelors around. He had actually come to Auschwitz as a volunteer when his mother had to go. He was one of the few people who had not been vulgarized by camp.

A-4116 asked him, *Why didn't you tell me about the chimneys the night I arrived?*

To what end? I knew you would find out soon enough, and besides, I'm firmly convinced we will survive. God knows I have no rational explanation for what I believe, but somehow, I know it won't be the same this time. There could be an uprising. Maybe we could burn down the whole place, but I can assure you that no one will go quietly to the gas chambers singing the national anthem like they did in March. We're too young to die without a fight, and something will be organized before that cursed deadline. Just keep your mouth shut and be careful. There are spies all around. Don't trust anyone, even people you've known for a long time. People have changed here.

Lost in thought, A-4116 walked out into the sunshine toward Kitty's block.

Well, look who's here. Nazdar. Two young men she used to dance with in her teens stood in front of her, grinning, one a former salesman in a fabric shop in Prague.

Still the well-dressed young lady, said Willy.

Yeah, and a grass widow in the bargain, Mirko pitched in.

How do you like our lovely village?

I bet that being as smart as you are, you managed not to let the Cripo rob you clean. What did you manage to bring in?

Not much, really, just a couple of watches, but I don't want to sell anything right now if that's what you're after.

If you keep that in your bunk, you won't have it very long, remarked Mirko. *They find everything in time.*

Don't you two worry about me. They're well put away, and you can bet your life that I won't tell YOU *where. See you.*

She continued on her way to Block 4, where Sylva,* one of the prettiest girls of Prague, was *Capo.* Always a spoiled brat and incredibly stupid, she took her function quite seriously and ran her block like the ruler of a good-sized duchy, regarding the inmates as her loyal subjects. Oddly enough, many of them seemed to go along with this fiction.

As her knight and lover she had Heini, a *Capo* in another part of Auschwitz who came to Birkenau regularly with deliveries of provisions. He was a criminal from Hamburg, serving a sentence of ninety-nine years for armed robbery. Aside from this disturbing aspect of his personality, he had a heart of gold and was a truly fine human being. He was well liked by the SS and was a frequent guest at their drinking sprees. Gifted with natural diplomatic skills, he had a way of drawing them out about their plans and intentions for Birkenau.

He was one of the best sources of information for the camp, not only in matters of immediate concern, but for news of the war. Fortunately, he was friendly with some male prisoners as well, because his tidings often got warped beyond recognition in Sylva's retelling. Kitty suggested that A-4116 see Sylva to arrange a transfer to Block 4, but after watching the scene for ten minutes, she tactfully declined and preferred to stay perched above the old ladies in Block 12 with Nina. This was going to be rather lonely, but better than becoming a lady-in-waiting at this ridiculous court.

One of the curiosities of Birkenau was the selection of its *Capos*. All of them were young. The SS ostensibly preferred to deal with pretty faces and good figures. So much for the women. The men were chosen mostly for their ability in playing soccer. The SS loved to watch it often, being too lazy or drunk to play it themselves. The *Cripos* were handpicked for their lack of scruples, after careful observation.

Another curiosity was the latrine. This was the meeting place of the camp, particularly in bad weather and during working hours. It was simply a ditch with four-by-four planks on each side, one for men, the other for women, with no partition. A fairly good sense of balance was required in order not to fall in. After a while, one learned to recognize friends by their naked rear ends. Toilet, or any other, paper was a memory. Opposite the planks were tin sinks with water faucets, and this comprised the entire sanitary facilities for the ten thousand prisoners. The water from the sinks drained into the ditch and so formed a very efficient arrangement.

Still wanting more information about the events of March, A-4116 went to see Nina one night.

How is it that you and a few others are still here from the December transport?

Didn't anybody tell you that Mother and I both had typhoid fever? Nina replied. *It's as simple as that. I don't want to talk about it. What else do you want to know?*

Why is there only one woman in Birkenau with her hair shaved off, while in the neighboring compounds all of them have shaved heads?

All the women in Auschwitz have shaved heads except the Capos and the inhabitants of Birkenau. Now, with Sarah, the Capo of Block 2, it's a special story. Quite funny, if you can still laugh at it. You know how difficult it is to get together with a man in this place, even if you happen to be a Capo. So she and her husband decided that the kitchen would be a good place to use as a refuge for a little lovemaking after morning Appell. It was lovely for a while, but suddenly they were rudely interrupted by one of the SS men, who had unexpectedly decided on a spot check of the kitchen. Her husband was lame for weeks from the beating he received, and she had to have her hair shaved off.

You'll find out that the Germans are inventive when it comes to their personal entertainment. Take the kids. I mean the boys between twelve and fifteen. It's a disaster for them if they're pretty. All Hitler's race laws don't prevent the SS from keeping them around their barracks, feeding them all kinds of goodies, and giving them license to do as they please as far as the other prisoners are concerned. Just as long as they're blond and blue-eyed. Sometimes when they get tired of playing with them, they hang or shoot them for the fun of it, but mostly they send them back to the men's barracks, where they are impossible to manage. Sylva's brother, Eddie, is a "peeple"—that's what they call the boys. It's late. Are you hungry? Here, have a piece of salami, but don't let the others see it. Go to sleep. Go.

18

T he next morning, before the main soup break, Eddie came into the workshop. Standing in front of A-4116, he announced, *Cripo Schlesinger wants you in his office. Step on it.*

Arriving, she found that striped clown sprawled behind a desk.

So you think you can get around me? Where are those Swiss watches? You do realize that it is illegal to hide valuables from the authorities. Or don't you?

Of course I know that, but I'm not hiding anything. If you don't believe me, why don't you send someone over to search my bunk or frisk me here?

You are a liar and you know it, but I'll teach you. First we'll shave off your head and maybe then you'll remember the truth.

While screaming these threats, his own bald head getting redder and redder, the door opened and in walked Willy and Mirko, her former dance partners, with a few pieces of jewelry they had found on an old woman in Nina's block, where they had been sent to search for A-4116's treasure. An argument ensued among the three as to how the loot would be divided, and realizing that for the moment she was forgotten, A-4116 slipped out the door and returned to her workshop, happily caressing her tresses. Hopefully, Schlesinger's head would cool off and he would leave her alone.

After this experience, A-4116 retreated into her own private world populated with people from the past, and nurtured wild fantasies of escape. This retreat naturally and very quickly earned her a reputation for arrogance and snobbishness. She spent the hours of the night before sleep working out meticulous plans for an escape. She would somehow have to find some insulated wire cutters, cut holes into the barbed wire, make her way to the railroad ramp, and hide in the underbelly of a cattle car until it left. If the Count of Monte Cristo could get out of Devil's Island, she would get out of here.

With daylight came the terrible awareness of the impossibility of these pipe dreams. Other nights, she spun out endless fantasies about a platonic love affair she had had at the age of seventeen that ended with the emigration of the young man. Now she imagined the wildest love scenes that had never taken place, feeling his arms around her, even smelling the scent of his pipe. Strangely enough, her husband never played a role in these sexual fantasies. She did miss Joe. He would have been good to have around, if only to keep away hooligans like Mirko and Willy.

She also found that she was becoming totally incapable of feeling pity or concern for the old ladies living with her and became very impatient with their sometimes naive questions. She was also always looking for ulterior motives when someone offered a favor or asked for one. The only people she still trusted were Kitty, Honza, Gisa, and Aunt Hella, a cousin of Mutti's whom she had discovered here in Block 2.

But even with them she kept a protective distance—for different reasons in each case. She went to see them occasionally, and left feeling lonelier than before. She was hungry most of the time, but did not go to see Honza too often for fear of being thought a beggar, knowing that he was one of the rare men in camp who did not demand, much less expect, any kind of payment. Flirting and necking had here evolved into outright prostitution for food. Far from being critical of many of her contemporaries, she just felt she hadn't sunk deep enough for that.

She had always loved Aunt Hella, but her likeness to Mutti was too much to bear for any length of time and she fled from her well-meant interest and concern. She knew very well that Gisa needed her more than ever, but suddenly could find nothing to talk about with the child. Gisa must have felt this too, as their walks together became fewer and fewer. Even Kitty was becoming a different person in her eyes, with her fear verging on paranoia. Kitty was in the midst of their old crowd from Prague, the girls she had rejected because of their kowtowing to Sylva but now sometimes longed to belong to.

May became June, and the camp atmosphere grew tenser and more hostile with every day. The SS were stepping up their favorite entertainment, which was to have anywhere from fifty to a few hundred prisoners report for calisthenics. They would order push-ups, knee bends, and running in place until at least half dropped from exhaustion. Each prisoner that fell added to their nefarious amusement, proving the theory of the inferiority of the Jewish race.

The signal that the camp was waiting for was the distribution of postcards to be sent to friends and relatives in Terezín. This had happened in March, when the condemned were made to write that they were well and working. The postcards were postdated March 25, while the people were actually disposed of on March 7. Because the March *Aktion* had taken place exactly six months after the arrival of the September transport, it followed by simple arithmetic that the people who had arrived in December would go in June. Both transports had come with the designation *Rückkehr Unerwünscht* (Return Undesired). Most of the May people tended to be more optimistic, simply because they had not lived through that particular catastrophe, and mass hysteria had not yet taken complete hold of them in the short weeks they had been in Auschwitz. The whole idea still sounded preposterous to them, in spite of all the evidence to the contrary.

Anxiety peaked when postcards were actually distributed on June 10, 1944. The prisoners had to write *Birkenau* and their name and birthdate as a return address. It was impossible to convey anything of consequence in the limited number of words permitted, and evidently even prearranged codes were misunderstood back in the ghetto. Even if the rumors of Auschwitz had reached them, the name Birkenau had no meaning or association for them. According to an agreement with her friends that she would write the exact opposite of what she meant, A-4116 wrote, *I am fine. Wish you were here.* Considering the later fate of Terezín's population, these messages did not accomplish anything at all.

The planning and plotting inside Birkenau went into high gear; rebellion and fury hung in the air. One young inmate, an excellent sportsman and youth leader, broke down and walked into the charged wires one week later, when sacks filled with replies arrived from Terezín. The camp was now ordered to write new cards dated June 2.

On June 18, Heini the burglar arrived with some startling information: the treatment of Jews was to undergo a drastic change. He claimed that the order had come directly from Berlin—from Göring himself. The new idea was not to kill Jews capable of work, but rather send them to places with acute labor shortages and let nature take its course.

Heini implored everyone to calm down; there would be a selection in the next few days in which people between fifteen and forty years of age would be chosen to be sent away to work camps. He warned that women with children would be excluded as well as the older and younger groups, but argued that this was better than a rebellion. That had no chance of success at all and would only annihilate the whole camp. He was understandably elated that his beloved Sylva would be saved, and had already made plans to escape and find and marry her if and when the Russian front would get close enough. She now had the problem of keeping her forty-four-year-old mother with her.

It all sounded too good to be true, but on June 20, 1944, the children's block was made ready for the first selection of men.

Dr. Mengele, the SS medical officer in charge, arrived and smilingly picked up a few small children to joke with. After this, the process of picking the strongest and healthiest men began. It took all afternoon, and when it was finished, the men selected were immediately marched out of the camp. Hours of anxious waiting followed. The pessimists still maintained that the whole thing was a ruse to get the able-bodied out of the way first because information about the planned rebellion had leaked out and reached the ears of the Germans.

Hours turned into days as the wives and mothers of the men took turns watching the visible railroad ramp to ascertain if their men were being put on a train. It appeared that the pessimists had been correct when on July 1 a large group of prisoners with bald heads and brand-new gray prison uniforms emerged on the ramp. A little girl posted as a lookout gave the signal and half of the female camp population raced dangerously close to the wire fences to see if these were really their men. The distance was too great to be able to recognize individual faces, but seeing the crowd, the men looking toward the camp started to wave and blow kisses. In tears the women watched the loading of the train and saw it leaving.

During the early afternoon of the same day, the procedure was repeated with the women. A thunderstorm was coming up, and it was getting darker and darker as some 2,500 women massed in the children's block. They crowded at one end in frightened silence, while at the other Dr. Mengele stood, arms crossed over his decorated chest, in shining black riding boots, with his aides and scribes. Someone barked an order to strip to the skin and to put clothes

over the left arm. A parade began in single file. At arrival in front of
the doctor, each woman had to come to attention and answer several
questions. Afterward, Mengele indicated with a slight movement of
his thumb to move to the right or left side of the hall. Very soon, a
pattern emerged: the group on the left was clearly intended for the
chimneys, since it included all the weak, old-looking, spectacle-
wearing, or scarred persons. The storm was now directly above us.
The thunder and lightning made the scene—a few thousand naked
women standing in front of twenty booted Germans in green
uniforms—look like the fantasy of an insane surrealistic painter.

A-4116 watched the proceedings with her detached interest,
making a mental note of the fact that even young and strong girls
with appendectomy scars wound up on the wrong side; that by
some strange coincidence everybody had become a dressmaker,
factory or farm worker overnight; and that every last housewife
had disappeared. When she reached the dashing doctor, he fired
the questions at her.

Number?

A-4116.

Age?

Twenty-four.

Married?

Yes.

Children?

Yes.

Profession?

Electrician.

What? Electrician? Is that true?

Yes.

YOU know how to pull wires and such?

Yes.

To the right—and make a note of that, he ordered the scribe.

Happy, she joined Kitty, who had already made it there, and pulled on her clothes. The other girls crowded around, wanting to know what had caused the change of pace in the metronomic rhythm of the proceedings. A-4116 explained in whispers that the idea of declaring herself an electrician had come to her on the spur of the moment, when she was frantically thinking of something original to distract the eyes of the doctor from the appendectomy scar on her belly. It wasn't an outright lie, since her father was an electrical engineer and had always encouraged her to learn how to fix faulty wiring or an appliance at home.

In any event, she said, this would be forgotten tomorrow, and for now, it had served its purpose very well. Many others had lied during this long afternoon, especially about their age and occupation, more or less successfully. Only one denied that she had a child—a four-year-old boy who was born when she was only seventeen—and no one had the nerve to criticize her for that. She could not have helped him, even if she stayed with him.

That evening after the selection, leave-taking was hard for the lucky ones picked to go. A-4116 went first to see Aunt Hella, her last link to the older generation. She found her in a serene mood, with not a trace of fear of her assured death. They sat with their arms about each other, the young one tongue-tied, just soaking up the warmth of the motherly woman, while the older one echoed Mutti's parting words, encouraging her to stay strong and try her best to stay alive. Hella told her not to pity her, that this was the one thing she could not take, and told her of the beautiful life she had had and the many happy times with Mutti. It all sounded so strangely familiar.

On the way back she met Gisa, making her way to Block 12 with a pair of shoes A-4116 had given her in Terezín when she had outgrown hers. Gisa was barefoot. Together they entered the block and sat on the bunk holding hands while Gisa explained that she had brought the shoes because they were much better than the ones A-4116 had acquired after foolishly swapping her boots, which had never been returned. *I won't need them anymore*, she said. *Right?*

There was no answer for this child who understood the score only too well, even though the grown-ups had tried all along to keep the truth from her. Gisa was now thirteen, but physically not developed enough to pass for a fifteen-year-old and so not even eligible for the selection. A few girls her age had slipped through the net as well as a dozen or so young-looking women over forty, but "A concentration camp is no kindergarten" was the slogan of the rulers. The goodbyes were said, and the ones about to leave went to sleep with a heavier heart than the ones to be left behind. The thunder and lightning had stopped and all was quiet.

19

The following morning before *Appell*, the chosen women were called out from their barracks by number and name. They were marched off at a brisk pace some two kilometers and arrived at a huge compound with the sign KONZENTRATION-SLAGER A I FRAUENLAGER.

This camp was much larger and more crowded than Birkenau. The barracks were built of stone. The roads were in better shape, although the base was the same ocher-colored loam, but here they were dotted with rough cobblestones. Instead of the male SS guards, SS women were very much in evidence. The prisoners here wore raggedy striped uniforms and generally looked much more decimated than the girls from Birkenau. The exception were the *Capos* and their deputies, who looked positively well fed and clean, with their long hair worn in ponytails caught with neat black bows. The same could be said about the young teenage runners, who were the exact counterpart of the *peeples* in Birkenau. It was almost impossible not to be reminded of a pet Pekinese or poodle when observing them.

Most of the rank and file had shaved heads or very short hair, just beginning to grow in. Walking was seemingly forbidden, since everybody was constantly running. Counted off by groups of five hundred, the newcomers were herded into low, Russian-style barracks with tiny windows. Inside, instead of bunks there were long shelves about five feet deep against the walls and another similar construction running through the center. There were no pallets, no blankets, and no straw. They were chased up into these cage-like contraptions with a flood of curses and shoves from the Polish *Capos* and strictly admonished to stay there or else.

The *Capos* seemed to be absolutely incapable of speaking in a normal tone, much less to be talked to or asked a question. Every shouted sentence was preceded by a curse. *You Czech whores who think that you are different!* Or, *Dirty Jew bitches, who deserve to drown in their own shit, we'll teach you what Auschwitz is all about! You haven't seen anything yet.* All this in Polish, which many understood but few spoke. All got the meaning anyway.

No sooner were they packed in than they were chased out to stand *Appell.* This time, a number of individuals were called out by their numbers and taken away for reasons no one understood until later. Twins were taken out for medical experiments Dr. Mengele was running in the camp hospital; also nurses and some others who were supposed to stay in A I for reasons they did not know.

Various SS women came and went, inspecting the rows standing at attention. Talking was forbidden. One of the SS caught a girl whispering to her neighbor and made her kneel on the stony ground, her arms lifted above her head, and then placed a heavy rock in each hand. Every time her arms relaxed a little, a guard or *Capo* would yell at her to stretch them out or else. This went on for hours. Finally when *Appell* was over, the girl had to be held up on both sides by her friends. Her knees would not carry her.

Next, a dozen stools were brought and their hair was cut. It came as a pleasant surprise that our hair was not shaven, but just cut short to the ears. That seemed like a good omen, considering that it's easier to shave a live body than a dead one. If they were destined for the gas, the reasoning went, all of it would have come off for the German arts and crafts shop. There was a good deal of scuttling and regrouping during the relatively less guarded period of the haircutting, with the effect that a few girls, including Kitty and A-4116, succeeded not only in saving their manes but also managed to form a cluster that vowed to stay together come what may. Even having seen the men leave, many still did not trust the accuracy of Heini's information.

After all these hours everybody had the desperate need to go to the latrine, and groups of ten were relayed there by *Capos*. The time spent there was strictly rationed, and whoever took too long in the view of the escort was poked in the buttocks with a pitchfork. This was accompanied by a flood of invective utilizing every filthy word contained in three languages. With the echo of the favorite curse *Cholera should take you!* they were chased back to their barracks to stand for another long *Appell*. At last they were given a mugful of black liquid called coffee and a slice of bread and locked inside the barrack.

With darkness, another kind of assault materialized in the form of the biggest bedbugs ever seen by anyone present. They were the size of fully grown cockroaches, and they attacked without mercy. The shelves were so overcrowded that sleep was only possible sandwiched like spoons between one's neighbors. When one turned, the whole row of some fifty people had to turn as well. A-4116 had always been irresistible to bugs of any kind, and was now so bitten up that she could not sleep at all. Disregarding the order not to leave the bunks, she slid down in the darkness to the stone floor, where she found a barrel covered by a blanket. She pulled it over herself and, feeling warm and comfortable, dozed off. The next morning, she slept so soundly that Kitty and a few others had to spend a considerable time bringing her back to consciousness. The barrel contained chlorine and the blanket was soaked full of its gases.

The next day, the group was taken under armed guard to a different section of Auschwitz where the other Birkenauers were already assembled in front of a building marked SAUNA. This immediately revived our anxieties since it was well known that the gas chambers were camouflaged by this title. There were flower beds all around, and to A-4116, the bright red of the begonias looked positively obscene against the dismal gray of the windowless building. Still outside, in full view of their escort of SS men, they were ordered to strip and throw their clothes and shoes onto two separate piles.

Hysteria flaring up here and there around them, the two cousins stood silently holding hands. Two by two, they were slowly let into a room where a big, fat SS woman stood in front of a dirty surgical table with stirrups, a white coat thrown over her uniform. Brutally she inspected every single one of our orifices without once changing her rubber glove. One of the girls, determined to save a souvenir from her lover, clutched a few buttons of his coat in her hand. Realizing that there was absolutely no place to hide them, she finally swallowed the keepsakes.

The next stop in the processing were the showers. Groups of one hundred were let in at a time. The orders were: one minute of water; one minute of soaping, with a piece of ersatz soap distributed to each foursome; one minute to rinse; and no noise. Hesitantly, the herd entered the shower room, prodded by guards and *Capos*, peering with unspeakable horror at the showerheads reputed to carry gas as well as water.

Sh'ma Israel Adonai Eloheinu was heard in a whisper. An eternity seemed to pass. Then a hissing sound from overhead: water! Boiling-hot water! A shout of relief went up, and the whole scene changed to a mad ballet in an effort to avoid the scalding streams. Coming out on the other side, each woman was given a pair of underpants and a gray prisoner shift and ordered to pick shoes from the pile outside.

This was practically impossible. How could anyone find her shoes in a mixed-up pile? The result was too ridiculous for words, but the fights that broke out when one person found her shoes on someone else's feet were not.

Another long *Appell* and the *Lagerkommandant* arrived for inspection. A-4116 stood in the first row when the lady slowly started her review. The command *Achtung!* was given, but A-4116, who had already recovered some of her natural sass, neglected to take her hands out of her pockets.

The *Kommandant* stopped in front of her. *Hands out of your pockets, Jew bitch!* A blow flat across the face with the back of her ringed hand came almost simultaneously. The prisoner's hands flew forward for her throat, but Kitty and another girl already held her elbows so tightly that she could not move. The group was ordered to march out of A I in the direction of the ramp.

After being provided with a piece of bread each, the group was loaded into rather clean cattle cars with fresh straw. To their delight and surprise, the doors remained open about a foot, and after some more delays and shouted commands, the train started to move. Slowly gathering speed, it took at least twenty minutes to get out of the Auschwitz complex. The administration buildings formed a little town in itself. Only in broad daylight did one get an idea of the immensity of this death factory. Countless square compounds separated by barbed-wire fences were dotted with watchtowers, and from the train, the inmates seemed like crawling ants.

Then, quite suddenly, the view changed. Moving in a western direction, the train passed through flowering meadows with bubbling brooks: lush, green, totally unbelievable. The sight of farmers working in the fields, grazing cattle, and ordinary people just going about their business brought us a sudden awareness that there was a life to be lived after all and that maybe soon one would be part of it again. It was the fourth of July. The sun was brilliant in the sky, the smoke of Auschwitz was receding in the distance, and someone started to sing:

> *The world is ours.*
> *There's room for every one*
> *and on the ruins of the ghetto we will laugh.*

It was a song from a prewar avant-garde revue that had been adapted for Terezín, and was a favorite among all Czech prisoners. Song followed song, and after running through the repertory of Czech pop and folk songs, we sang "Old Man River" and "Anchors Aweigh." The scene was reminiscent of a youth hostel trip. Empty stomachs were forgotten; the women laughed, teased, and tickled each other like an exuberant bunch of kids intoxicated with the sheer joy of living. Even the armed escorts riding in the cabin of each car could not suppress a smile.

20

The doors of the cars were locked when the train neared the more industrial regions of Germany. But not even this could dampen the girls' high spirits. A-4116 and Kitty were surrounded by girls from Prague, with a sprinkling from the provinces. They belonged to the same generation and had known each other long before the emergence of Adolf Hitler. Bound by their recent experiences, they swore to try to stay together and help each other.

A very strange scene awaited the travelers the next evening when the train slowed down and, finally, ground to a halt in Hamburg. It stopped in front of a dark row of buildings three stories high, with huge sliding doors on every floor.* Those doors and the windows were hung like vines with young men! Boys of every shape and size,

---

* Editor's note: This was Dessauer Ufer, a sub-camp of the Neuengamme concentration camp located inside the port of Hamburg, in operation from July 1944 until April 1945. It was the first sub-camp for women in Neuengamme.

wearing unfamiliar uniforms without insignia, were laughing and shouting all at the same time, obviously delighted with the arrival of a trainload of young women.

The ladies were puzzled, then smiled back and waved. Car after car was unloaded under the supervision of an extremely handsome and elegant SS *Hauptscharführer*, who was instantly christened Petrovich,* after a popular German movie star. The women were divided into two groups and sent up into what had been a warehouse for river barges with loading facilities on both sides. One side of the building faced the tracks, and the other side was directly on the water.

Inside the warehouse were several round openings like manholes, with thick ropes for pulleys, and rows of bunks arranged in blocks of six. On the track side was a low sink with many water faucets in the center, and a partitioned corner reserved for the *Capo*. The whole place was dark and cavernous and, even in the summer, very cold. The Czech group dashed to the opposite windows to stake out claims to a row of bunks. Some immediately climbed on a bench to look out.

The boys next door, having had the same idea, were already crowding their windows, and introductions did not take long. There were some initial language problems since they were all Italians—either deserters from Mussolini's army or captured partisans who had fought with Tito against the Fascists. Many of them spoke some French or broken German. On the Czech side, German, French, and rusty school Latin had to serve.

Meanwhile, another group of the new arrivals started a veritable water orgy at the other end of the hall. Naked, they sprayed each other from the faucets, holding fingers against the pressure, completely oblivious to the fact that for several minutes Petrovich had been standing in the doorway with a group of guards, watching the scene. One by one, as they became aware of the men's stares, the girls disappeared into the bunks, until only Sylva was standing on top of the sink like a marble nymph. Chuckling, Petrovich ordered her down and to the *Kommando* quarters two floors below. One can only guess at what happened there, but Sylva did not seem to be upset by the episode and certainly did not look maltreated on her return.

The boys next door had abandoned their positions the moment they discovered the presence of the guards, but returned in full force with the falling darkness. Unfortunately, there was only one window that was close enough to enable a conversation, with room for not more than three at a time, so turns had to be taken.

This immediately led to fights about whose turn and for how long. The group nearest to the window established a monopoly, doling out space and time as special favors. There had been a tall blond man in the door of the Italian house when they arrived who had focused his eyes on A-4116 from the moment the train had pulled in. They were now talking together, explaining their circumstances. His name was Bruno and he came from northern Italy. Unable to chat for any length of time, since turns had to be taken, he asked her to come back to the window later, mentioning something about having an idea.

After her return from Petrovich, Sylva had to get in on the fun and immediately struck up a mad love-affair-at-first-sight with a Roman named Flavio. They could hardly communicate, but just looked deeply into each other's eyes and sighed *Flavio* and *Sylva* over and over again—a situation that quickly became boring to everyone not immediately involved, particularly since all this took place twenty yards apart and at least forty feet above sea level.

When A-4116 returned to the window, there was Bruno with a little package tied to a long laundry rope, which he started to swing parallel to the building until she was able to catch it. The system worked beautifully, and the next hour was spent in this highly satisfying activity. At least fifty girls acquired "their" Italian that night. The package A-4116 received contained a comb, toothbrush, cigarettes, a pencil, a pair of socks, chocolate, paper, and a long letter that read something like this:

Dear Francesca,

When the train that brought you pulled up in front of our prison today, my heart went out to all of you. You looked so scared and lost and so young and pretty at the same time. It has been a long time since we saw some pretty girls. I spotted you even before the train stopped and could not tear myself away from the expression in your eyes. What have they done to you, and where did you come from? My name is Bruno, as you know by now, and I come from Treviso, not a very big city. I have eleven brothers and sisters and I miss them very much. When the war broke out I was drafted in the Army, but I never liked the Blackshirts and soon I fled across the water to Yugoslavia with a group of friends to join the partisans. One day we were captured by the Germans and sent here to work. The work is hard, but we are treated quite well and can write home and receive packages. My friends here think that you are all wonderful, and we will help you as much as we can. But you are special for me. I think I love you and I want to marry you when the war is over. You would like it in Italy. It is so beautiful there. We would have many little bambini, and I would make you very happy. Please don't answer me right away because this must be a surprise to you, but maybe soon you will love me too. I can take care of you and the bambini very well. I have a very good job with a furniture factory, and because I know French, I will surely work in the export section after the war. The Americanos have landed in France, and we will be free and happy soon. I am sending you a few things because I saw that you had nothing with you, but mostly paper, so that you can write me long letters telling me all about you. I have to finish because time is short and you have to sleep. I will wait in the window tomorrow night, mia cara piccola bambina. *I would like to kiss you, but you are too far but very near too.*

Your Bruno

The feeling of being recognized as a woman was warm and beautiful, especially since she felt anything but pretty at the moment. The toothbrush and chocolate were shared with Kitty—as well as the letter, of course.

The commotion eventually subsided, and no sooner had they fallen asleep than an alert sounded and, ten minutes later, all hell broke loose. The nightly bombardment of Hamburg had begun. This observer sat cross-legged on her bunk, Kitty's head buried in her lap, in an eerie state of elation. Every flare that burst in the sky and the subsequent crash of an exploding bomb made her feel more exhilarated. Below her, eighteen-year-old Marion was kneeling, reciting one Ave Maria after the other. Others had pulled their blankets over their heads to muffle the noise, but for A-4116 there could not be enough of it and she was sorry when the all clear sounded. This was a very strange reaction from someone who since childhood had been afraid of shooting and who used to hold her hands over her ears in the last act of *Tosca* because she could not bear to hear a shot. It just proved again that she had really left her old self.

The night was disturbed only one more time, when a rat ran over Gerti's* face, reducing her to hysterics. Rats were big and plentiful, being so near the waterfront, and hungry too, since there were now humans living where grain used to be stored. At five a.m. reveille sounded, and after putting on the flimsy, drab overalls issued the night before and sloshing down some black coffee, the girls lined up in front of the building. Broken up into groups of twenty with two guards to each section, they marched off singing a Sousa march toward another canal, where they boarded a steamer to take them to various places of work.

In contrast to Auschwitz, the guards were now older members of the Wehrmacht, unfit for front duty. Some of them, to be sure, were ambitious zealots taking their duty with deadly seriousness and could be very unpleasant. Most were much less vicious than the SS men they had learned to fear.

It was chilly on the boat that early in the morning, and A-4116 huddled against the chimney trying to get warm. One of the men running the old crate came up laughing at her hopeless attempts to light a cigarette in the strong breeze.

You are not a sailor, I see, he said, and taught her how to cup her hand and light the match and cigarette with one flick of his wrist.

He then wanted to know who they were and where they came from. When told that they were Jewish prisoners his friendliness froze and he vanished in a hurry.

From the water, one could see the devastation of this once-beautiful city. Whole city blocks were only piles of rubble. Smoke rose to the sky from burning oil tanks after the bombardment of the preceding night. The lovely rich suburb of Blankenese gleamed curiously untouched atop the palisades of the river. The boat docked at an oil refinery called Erdoel, and here the work detail debarked. The prisoners were given shovels as far as they were available and assigned to clear the rubble from the air attacks into huge piles. They were also instructed to report any unfamiliar object found to the guard, so that a Russian POW detail could be called to deal with it in case it was an unexploded shell.

The refinery was still working, even though many of the buildings and tanks were in ruins. There were slave laborers of every nationality of occupied Europe everywhere. The POWs were mainly French, but also Russians, who were in the most pitiful state, obviously starving and dressed in the torn rags that had once been their uniforms. They were too downtrodden to communicate with anyone, and their guards also treated them with exceptional cruelty.

The rest were civilian forced workers from all over. Communication with the French was quickly established when the guards looked the other way, or in the latrines, where knots in the wood were conveniently pushed out to make conversation easier. This very soon led to a lengthy, rather good-natured tirade by a Bavarian guard who could not understand why it took us so long to tinkle: *What are you girls doing in there for such a long time? When I have to piss I run in like a young stag, take a leak, and out again. Well, what can one expect of women?*

The French POWs understood the situation right away, having the longest experience with the system, and helped as much as they were able. They were considerably better off than us because under the rules of the Geneva Convention, they were allowed to receive packages and money. They were also not afraid to take risks to help, whereas the civilian laborers trembled before anyone in a German uniform. The German workers completely ignored everybody, making it their business to look the other way when faced with a group of foreigners or prisoners.

The work was hard, and harder still for women who had never held a shovel in their hands before. It took days to learn the trick of swinging a full shovel up onto a truck, and some never learned. A-4116 rather enjoyed the work once she mastered the movement and was often accused by her coworkers of working too hard. But for her restless nature, that was better than to lean on her shovel and brood about the past or the uncertain future. Besides, one kept warmer that way.

The picking up and loading of broken bricks was not any easier. A chain was formed from pile to truck with the shards passed from hand to hand, and after an hour of this, everyone's fingertips were bleeding.

Relief came at noon when a truck from the "German People's Welfare" drove up with barrels of thick soup based mainly on turnips and potatoes. It tasted vile but was hot and filling, at least for a few hours. By comparison with Auschwitz, a vast improvement.

Kitty had acquired a French friend during the morning who soon slipped her a piece of bread and a little note with a promise of more to come when she met him the following day at the latrine. He was a Parisian by the name of Pierre, smiling and winking at her whenever he passed by. At six p.m., the whistle sounded and a very tired column shuffled back to the boat for the return trip, a good deal of the elation of the last few days gone.

On their return, there were long lines for a bowl of watery soup and a piece of bread, after which most of the girls collapsed exhausted on their bunks, cursing their sore feet and aching muscles. Bruno and his friends were already waiting at their windows, and the scene of the previous night repeated itself in a somewhat less rambunctious tone. This time he threw over a sweater after having watched A-4116 shiver at *Appell* in the morning.

She wrote him a letter thanking him for his gifts and his very touching proposal, but also told him that the idea of marriage was problematic, because as far as she knew she was already married. It was a calculated risk to tell the truth; it could easily have cut off Bruno's much-needed help, but the sincerity of his first letter left really no alternative. He took the news philosophically, resolved to treat her like a sister from now on, and a very strong friendship developed.

21

T he bombardment of the first night repeated itself every other night with clocklike precision, with the difference that now, at the sound of the sirens, the women were chased out of their bunks and herded into the cellar, which served as an air-raid shelter. It slanted toward the water, and since the canal rose and fell with the tides, it was often half-submerged. It was cold there, and they sat shivering on the ground in total darkness with the rats scampering over their legs. Hearing only the sounds of explosions above, they were more uneasy than they had been upstairs at the thought of how to get out in case of a direct hit. The two cousins hated the cellar and, whenever possible, hid under their bunk.

The only advantage the cellar had was that it was connected by arched openings with the adjoining buildings below water level at high tide. This opened up interesting possibilities at ebb tide, which took several weeks to utilize. Meanwhile life fell into a routine. Hunger ever present, but alleviated with the help of the French and

Italians. Lack of sleep made everyone grouchy, and all remnants of courtesy and consideration fell by the wayside.

Envy of the foreign boyfriends on the part of those who had none accounted for a good deal of tension, and language became a gutter jargon. This led to a splitting up into groups of anywhere between two to six, which called themselves communes and looked out for their members. Violent arguments between these clusters were the order of the day. Curiously, very few people became ill—even common colds were rare. Whatever sick calls there were, were mostly minor accidents at work.

A month after their arrival, Petrovich was driving down the road on the opposite side of the canal and noticed the strange goings-on at the waterside of *his* storehouse. A-4116 was blithely hanging out the window when a powerful slap on her rear interrupted an interesting conversation with Bruno. Irritated, she turned around to see who the joker was and stared straight into Petrovich's cold eyes. Pulling her down, he was up on the stool in an instant, pulled out his revolver, and was shooting wildly in the direction of the Italians.

He could not do much harm because they all withdrew at high speed, but the event put an end to a marvelous mail service. Oddly enough, there were no other repercussions except for a stern lecture on the propriety of conduct for young ladies, with an admonition never to do it again. Why, the man had not totally lost his sense of humor after all.

Clearly, some other form of communication had to be found. Vera,* the *Capo* who did not go out to work with the rank and file, had an Italian boyfriend, who was the maintenance man for the whole complex of buildings and whom she had met when he came around to open some clogged drains. This Italian had succeeded in bribing the old German soldier who was often on day duty, and had become Vera's frequent visitor while the others were out at work. He now came to the aid of Bruno, Flavio, and the other boys and acted as letter carrier.

Sometime later, the old Kraut was put on night duty during the time of low tide, well before the usual alert. Taking advantage of such favorable conditions, the boys arranged for a meeting with their girls in the cellar at considerable cost and with painstaking planning. Only three had the guts to go along with that dangerous undertaking, and A-4116 made it a foursome after some initial reluctance. The night chosen was one when Petrovich was out on the town. After all the prisoners had gone to sleep, the German led the quartet quietly downstairs to the cellar. There, they had to promise to be back in one hour, because that was when the tide again began to rise. With a weak flashlight they picked their way through the knee-deep water into the next cellar, where the Italians were impatiently waiting.

Scattered and settled on higher ground in pairs, Bruno momentarily forgot his brotherly feelings and became very passionate. His partner did not exactly put up a stiff fight, but when it came to the moment of giving in completely, she froze rigid. All feelings drained away; she was suddenly only conscious of the dampness, the rats, and the utter ugliness of the situation.

With infinite tenderness, Bruno let go of her and, holding her in his arms, assured her of his understanding and love. When it was time to go, he kissed her hands and thanked her for coming. There were no hurt feelings, no reproaches about a missed opportunity, and their friendship became even stronger than before. Still, later she often regretted her lack of generosity. There must have been more of these meetings, but neither Bruno nor she made another effort to come together.

After discovering that there were identical openings leading out into the water, Bruno and Flavio hatched a plan whereby they, A-4116, and Sylva would swim to the opposite bank of the river, walk through Hamburg to the seaport, and convince a fisherman from neutral Sweden to take them out of the country.

The plan sounded possible but had several drawbacks. First, they had no contact with a Swede. He would have to be found on arrival, assuming that they could make it through Hamburg without attracting attention. Second, it would entail a separation from Kitty, and considering that the war was supposedly in its last stages, it did not seem worth it to risk drowning in the North Sea in case of a storm or a mine. After much discussion back and forth, the plan was rejected by all concerned.

Through Pierre, the cousins met another Frenchman, Marcel, who never brought them any food but passed whole bulletins of news through the holes in the latrine wall at Erdoel. He seemed to spend most of his nights glued to his self-built radio, listening to the BBC. He was a staunch Communist and argued that with the landing of the Americans in Normandy and the tide turning on the Russian front, it was only a matter of time before Germany would be ground up between two millstones.

The most important thing was to maneuver so that one would not be caught with the Germans. This was all very true, but did not change the day-to-day race for survival. The winter weather had started early, and the prisoners were freezing in their light overalls, their footwear in such a state that it became a full-time job to stuff their shoes with rags and paper in the attempt to keep dry feet. The older women started to show the effect of overwork, undernourishment, and lack of sleep. Sick calls multiplied, but more often they kept it secret for fear of being sent away.

Very few of them had help from the POWs, who were more attracted by the younger women. In desperation they took to scavenging in garbage piles and collecting cigarette butts, which they rerolled in whatever paper they could find and swapped for a piece of bread if they did not smoke it themselves. Not one of them was over fifty, but their endurance was eroding much faster than the stamina of the younger ones, who with the callousness of youth more or less disregarded their plight except when it came to their own mothers.

By the end of October 1944, rumor had it that they would be moved because the buildings were going to be reassigned for different use. Petrovich received orders to report to the front. The days of hinterland jobs for the SS were over. The Italians were to be given civilian status and integrated into the huge foreign labor force in the area.

Parting was sad. The boys provided their Czech friends with whatever they could spare and promised to stay in touch if they could ever discover where the girls were being taken. The result was tragicomic, for when they lined up to leave and Petrovich took a last review of his troops, they were all carrying bundles, although they had arrived four months earlier practically naked. Musing about this phenomenon, he stopped briefly in front of A-4116 and, pulling some cigarettes out of her breast pocket, asked, *Well, well now, where would these come from?*

I find them, Hauptscharführer.

You do? Where?

Every day in the same place, Hauptscharführer.

With that he shook his head, replaced them, and walked on. Loaded on trucks, the girls were taken to Neugraben, a suburb of Hamburg some fifteen miles away. Ten days later old Kraut told them that the storehouses on the canal had received a direct hit and had been leveled to the ground. The Italians had also been gone at the time.

22

Compared to all the previous places of detention, Neugraben was beautiful: a small camp with only four barracks set against a wooded area. But, alas, no visible neighbors except for the cluster of houses occupied by the new *Kommandant*.

He was an old man who looked like Captain Hook, but was actually a retired stationmaster hurriedly put into an SS uniform. His bark was worse than his bite, and he loved to give sermons at *Appell*, especially in the rain. Most of the old Wehrmacht guards had come along with us. Work was again clearing rubble and loading and unloading sand and bricks, but now the women were farmed out to different places each day and had to march anywhere from one to two hours each way.

They worked on the outskirts of Hamburg, sometimes in residential, middle-class neighborhoods, a circumstance that afforded more opportunity to "organize"—a euphemism for *steal*—all kinds of things in the half-destroyed houses on the way to and from their destinations. One could find all sorts of useless objects in the houses, seldom anything to eat. But one could dig for forgotten potatoes in the harvested fields one passed, or turnips. The guards were tired and did not pay too much attention when someone fell behind for a while.

One day one of the details passed an apple orchard on the way back to camp. There was some unpicked fruit still hanging on the trees, and in a second a few girls were up in them, throwing down apples to their comrades. By the time the group was brought back to camp, there had been a telephone complaint to the *Kommandantur* by the owner. This upset Captain Hook greatly, and outraged, he called an immediate *Appell*. Pent up with fury, he walked up and down the rows, unable to speak for a while, and then it came.

WHO has ever seen anything like THIS? JEW WENCHES on apple trees. Have you gone crazy? Hah, I will show you. YOU are going to swing LIKE SO from the trees. And then I'll shoot you personally. And then YOU'll be surprised and astonished.

The back rows were choking with laughter while the front row had to keep a straight face and the assembled guards broke out in uncontrollable fits of coughing.

From the German point of view the situation had seriously deteriorated, and some zealot sent in a report to the higher echelons. Only a few days later old Kraut told them that a dozen of the guards were being replaced by SS women and that Captain Hook would be exchanged for a new SS *Sturmbannführer*. The party was over.

The new *Kommandant* arrived a few days later with twelve SS women and made it immediately clear that he considered the state of the camp a stinky mess, and that reorganization would start forthwith. His name was Spiess.* He was a carpenter by trade, with a face like a squashed turnip and a mouth full of evil-smelling stumps, which caused a shower of spit to come out every time he spoke. He conducted his first *Appell* armed with his service revolver, plus a yard-length of rubber hose, which he swung around while introducing himself, warned that he would not hesitate to use it.

He had a passion for doing everything himself, or rather having the inmates do it. He was given to violent temper tantrums, during which foam would appear at his mouth like on a mad dog. The camp had a complicated system of bookkeeping, whereby it got paid for the labor performed by its inmates and, in turn, had to pay for food and other supplies. Hell-bent to streamline this obviously mismanaged outfit, Spiess's first act was to trim down the number of prisoners who stayed inside the camp for maintenance, and to scrupulously check the morning's sick calls to eliminate cheaters.

He retained Greta,* the top camp *Capo*, a former nightclub dancer from Berlin who had ended up here because she was married to a Czech Jew. She had ingratiated herself with Captain Hook by virtue of her *Berliner Schnauze* (Berlin attitude). Although pushing forty, she was just the type that was compatible with the overlords, and she succeeded in getting whoever she personally liked appointed as *Capos* and their deputies.

She was justified in one case. Her friend Mimi* was, at this juncture, five months pregnant, having conceived before she left Auschwitz. Mimi herself did not even know she was pregnant until the fifth month because almost all the prisoners had long since stopped menstruating, many of them after they entered the Industrial Palace in Prague. In itself, this was certainly no hardship. On the contrary. But it did not prevent conception, as many discovered too late. Greta now proposed that Mimi work for Spiess as a secretary, in order to keep her indoors during the cold winter months.

Unaware of the circumstances, he agreed, and quickly got used to her. Mimi was an excellent typist, so good that when Spiess eventually discovered her condition, he agreed to let her deliver the child in camp under the condition that it had to be disposed of the moment it was born. This was puzzling behavior from a man who was capable of beating inmates into unconsciousness for the slightest misdeeds. More so, in view of the very strict and explicit guidelines in regard to sick or pregnant prisoners: these had to be immediately dispatched to Bergen-Belsen. An SS medic visited the camp every two weeks for exactly that purpose, although it was ostensibly to check on the supplies for sick bay.

Not only did Spiess give Mimi an apple now and then, but he also locked her in a closet every time the medic came for inspection.

The second day after his takeover, while studying the papers gathering dust in his office, he discovered that there was an electrician among the inmates. A shout went out from block to block. *A-4116 to the Kommandantur! On the double!*

Expecting the worst, she was ushered into Spiess's office.

You are an electrician, he said, without looking up.

Yes, Sturmbannführer.

*I am moving this office to the other end of the barrack, where the
window looks out on the camp. I want this telephone moved there right
away. The cable is here in the corner. Verstanden?*

Jawohl.

He stalked out, leaving her without the faintest idea about how
to do it. Gingerly she unscrewed the wall box and made a diagram
of exactly how the wires were connected, using colored pencils
from his desk. Then she removed the box, connected the new cable,
isolated it, and drew it along the long corridor. She tacked it to the
wall, praying to the patron saint of electricians to make the damned
thing work. When she got to the other end of the barrack, she
remounted the box, connected the telephone, and picked up the
receiver in a cold sweat. A dial tone sounded just as Spiess returned
to see how far the work had progressed.

From that moment on, Spiess developed the ridiculous idea that
she could do almost anything. The next day, he decided to keep her
on as an indoor worker, with the title of Camp Maintenance
Woman—to the annoyance of Greta, who had to let go of one of
her protégées.

Next, Spiess decided that the food delivered for the *Kommandantur* from a central supply kitchen was not tasty enough. With
so many women around, it could be greatly improved, especially
since it would be possible to help himself to more provisions by
curtailing the camp allotment. The staff barracks had no kitchen—
one would have to be installed, and he and A-4116 would convert
a nearby dilapidated garage for just that purpose!

There was no electricity and therefore no light, also no stove and no chimney, but the latter was a minor detail he could not be bothered with now. First, the current had to be brought in from a high-voltage pole between the two buildings. He made complicated sketches with fuse boxes here and there, and produced some needed tools, but to A-4116 the whole project looked highly dangerous, since she was to do most of the work—albeit with Spiess's "expert" advice. What if by some mistake she burned the whole place down? Seeing no way out of the bind, she finally asked for some strong leather gloves so as not to electrocute herself.

On the first dry morning, Spiess arrived with a long ladder, and after taking off his own gloves and handing them over, he sent her up on the pole. Pulling together all her wits, she worked on that line the whole day, breaking the circuit twice by fuse boxes, and by evening, lo and behold there was actually light, although the cable swung dangerously in the wind.

The next day Spiess requisitioned a stove, pots, and pans, and commandeered the camp kitchen crew to cook for him and his staff under the supervision of a hefty SS woman named Erika.* In his view, the kitchen crew were just polishing their asses all day having to cook only coffee and one soup for some five hundred people.

After this, a grudging sort of respect for A-4116 came over Spiess, to the point that once, while sprawled behind his desk, feet on the table as she stood at attention receiving the day's orders, he growled, *At ease. Are you sure you are a Jewess?*

I wouldn't be here if I weren't, would I?

I've never heard of a goddamn filthy Jew working with his hands, yet you can. How so? Those parasites are only good for squeezing labor out of honest working men, or sitting around in cafés and plotting a Bolshevik revolution. Those rich Jew bankers even embroiled America into war with us. It's all in the Stürmer *every day. Well, say something! I'm not going to hit you.*

Sturmbannführer, I think you should not believe everything you read. Don't you know that there are millions of working Jews, some of them very poor? What about all the tailors, shoemakers, postmen, mechanics? And how do you figure that they can plot a Bolshevik revolution and be capitalists at the same time? Maybe things are not all black or white?

Nonsense. Fix that window here and then get to work. We haven't got all day.

Still shaking his head, he strode out of the room, carefully leaving one cigarette on the edge of the table. A-4116 shrugged her shoulders, trying to fathom Spiess, and got busy on his window.

There was plenty of work to do, particularly at the *Kommandantur.* The circuits were constantly overloaded by all the small appliances belonging to the SS women, and she spent hours in the low attic of their barrack, where all the wires were lying loose on the ceiling boards. Flat on her stomach, she fixed loose connections and short circuits. But she also killed a lot of time just daydreaming, or listening to the radio below, warm and dry and rather happy with her lot. According to the German newscasts, the Reich was victoriously pulling back on all fronts.

During November 1944, a shipment of coats from Bergen-Belsen finally arrived none too soon. The garments were old and had large yellow crosses painted with enamel on the backs. But the shoe situation continued to be a disaster. The girls walked in rags tied up with strings to work, and not even Spiess, with his warped sense of paternalistic concern for his prisoners, was capable of getting an allotment of even wooden sabots.

23

There were major problems with Kitty now. Somewhere in the rubble and filth, she had picked up a very itchy skin infection. She kept scratching and it developed into impetigo. Eventually, due to lack of vitamins and general malnutrition, she had full-blown furunculosis, covered with boils from head to foot. Some of them were so big they had to be lanced by the camp doctor, who, having been a young pediatrician before the war, did not have too much experience in surgery, and was handicapped by a dire shortage of bandages and disinfectants.

When Kitty developed boils in the glands of her armpits, she began to run a constant temperature that rose quite high. The doctor kept her inside for a few days at a time, but had to be careful. Spiess had the uncanny faculty of remembering faces at sick call and was liable to report anyone who did not seem to get well fast to the inspecting medic.

Kitty had been Room Elder of her dormitory; now, the other girls began to grumble about her cutting and touching their bread. This made her feel like a leper and sent her into an abyss of depression. It took some resourcefulness to get her out of these moods. A-4116 took to cleaning and dressing the endless abscesses and, to prove that she did not consider Kitty repulsive, started to sleep beside her under one blanket.

Greta took pity on her and talked Spiess into letting Kitty stay inside to clean the latrines. A-4116 tried in desperation to get a letter to Kitty's Christian fiancé in Prague. She was now officially permitted to walk the three hundred yards between camp and the *Kommandantur* without a guard and often encountered a German who wished her *Guten Tag*. This gave her the courage to stop one day, ask him to mail a letter to Prague, and bring back a reply in case there was one. She gave him ten of the two hundred marks that Bruno had given her, which she carried tied around her neck. He agreed and, in fact, came back some three weeks later with a small package of disinfectants, bandages, ointments, and a letter.

The letter did more for Kitty than the medicines (which were largely ineffective), for it proved to her that she was not forgotten. She carried it around with her, repeating its passages over and over, and for a while seemed to get better. Ivan's description of his never-ending love and yearning for her, as well as the news that his parents could not wait to have her back and were in fact redecorating a room of their house for her homecoming, was better therapy than what the camp doctor could provide.

The whole dorm shared the warmth and comfort of this loving message from home on the relatively quiet nights when power was often cut off by seven or eight p.m. Bombing alerts continued, but the bombs fell at a distance, and only the glow of the ensuing fires was visible. There was nothing to do in the cold and dark but to wrap up in the flimsy blankets and talk. They discussed the future, which seemed to be hidden in thick fog, and speculated about how many of them would be able to last to the end of the war. Not everyone was confident that things would automatically fall into place once the Nazis were beaten.

There was already widespread anxiety about just how they would cope with the demands of normal life: performing productive work, paying rent and gas bills, not to mention returning to mates who might not be the same men they had known. Many had acquired a slave mentality, living by their wits and ruses from day to day. An orderly or unregulated existence seemed utopian at this point.

The girls took long, imaginary walks through Prague, making it a game and awarding points to the ones who could best remember street names, stores, and many other details. The most popular and lush fantasy was of sitting in a hot bath.

A deep longing for Mutti overcame A-4116, and she started to write her letters in a notebook she had organized from Spiess's desk. Lying in the attic of the *Kommandantur*, supposedly working, she wrote down all that had happened since Mutti was taken away. She kept the book hidden inside her pallet in the hope of . . . what? She didn't know.

The duties of the indoor crew included the unloading of camp provisions and weekly trips to the outside to bring in bread and other supplies. These were holidays for the four girls assigned. The guard sat in the warm cab with the driver; the crew were high up on the open back of the truck, rejoicing in the general destruction around them.

When they arrived at the bakery, the guard immediately disappeared into the office for coffee and pastries, and the loading was left to the girls under the supervision of the bakery owner. Being the accomplished thieves they were by now, it did not take long to discover that the woman was not counting the loaves put on the truck—only the wooden boards on which they were carried out. Once the twenty loaves on each were emptied into the truck, the boards were stacked against the wall.

It was a cinch to put not only the bread but also the board up into the truck at a moment when the woman was distracted. On the way through the bakery, A-4116 also discovered some bricks of yeast stored on a shelf. She thought, *Vitamin B for Kitty*, and one of the bricks rapidly vanished under her coat. When the truck set out on its return trip, the girls had only two problems: disposing of the long wooden board on a crowded road and bringing into camp five loaves of bread each, without attracting attention to their suddenly expanded size.

The first problem was solved by throwing the plank overboard on a bridge across a canal; the second, by eating one loaf of bread right away. A-4116 was stuffing down the still-warm bread at such high speed that it suddenly got stuck in her esophagus and would not budge either way. Her face got red as a turkey, to the extreme entertainment of her pals, who massaged her frantically until the wad finally moved downward. The loot was brought in without a hitch, although Eva* claimed that the guard at the gate had given her a long and suspicious look.

For a few days the four and their respective communes went to sleep without their ever-present hunger pangs. The yeast did wonders for Kitty. It took the bakery woman four whole weeks to discover that she was always short of bread on the days the Neugraben camp came, and even then she had no proof, but she informed Spiess that she now had a truck available for deliveries.

This was sad news mainly because contact with the outside had become a matter of chance. No POWs worked in the area, and the civilian workers were stingy and scared. This left only the possibility of scavenging in the ruins, at which some girls had become virtuosos. Contact with the Italians had been lost completely, but a handful of girls had some Free French laborers who came to see them on some Sundays. Dita was once caught holding hands with her suitor through the barbed wire and was severely beaten by Spiess with his rubber hose. At *Appell* he held up the event as an example on moral grounds: it was unseemly for young girls to have secret meetings with Frenchmen. Evidently he was confusing a concentration camp with a nunnery.

24

A nother odd relationship came into being inside the camp, something quite usual and noticeable in A I in Auschwitz but not experienced as yet in the Czech group. A young SS woman called Bubi*, who was not only harmless but occasionally quite kind, became very friendly with Sylva. So friendly that she came often at night to visit, leaving at dawn. Sylva's roommates kept their mouths shut, and the subject was not widely discussed except for a few raised eyebrows among the more righteous. The fact was that neither Sylva nor her mother was very hungry from then on, and who was there to judge?

Out of the nightly rap sessions came the memories of the Liberated Theater in Prague and the highly improvised performances of its stars, Voskovec and Werich, who had been the idols of a whole generation of young people for their biting satirical revues and songs. Why not put together a show for Christmas? Some of the inmates had been professional singers, actresses, or writers, and there were lots of enthusiastic amateurs able and more than willing to get in on the fun.

Greta was won over and commissioned to secure permission from Spiess, as they wanted to use the mess hall for the project. Surprised, he consented under the condition that it had to be done in German, and that he and his staff had to see it first. A-4116 took on the technical side, and a committee was formed to write, stage, and direct various skits. A movable stage was built with tables and lights installed. Costumes were made from five hundred handkerchiefs that had just arrived as an allotment in place of shoes, and the SS women graciously offered some makeup supplies.

Annie,* who was a journalist on the staff of the *Prager Tagblatt* in Prague, wrote an original skit about an imprisoned princess (Kitty), her nurse (A-4116), and the white knight (Zdena*) who comes to her rescue and kills the Monster (to be played in the manner of a marionette moved from above on strings).

Another number was a scene from Schubert's *Dreimäderlhaus*, this mainly to satisfy the German taste for kitsch, starring the three camp beauties—Sylva, Eva, and Gerti—dressed in crinolines made of handkerchiefs. Greta did one of her nightclub routines, from twenty years before she became the respectable Mrs. Kohn, and A-4116 freely re-created the monologue play *The Human Voice* by Jean Cocteau that Vava had performed in Terezín. Poor Cocteau.

But the highlight of the production was Zdena, with a group of songs from operettas for the Germans and another one from the revues of V & W and other avant-garde anti-fascist composers. The whole production was an enormous labor of love with daylight hours for rehearsals in short supply and the problem of staging the entire show in two languages. They did not have the slightest intention of making the Czech version as tame as the German one.

Rehearsals were held on two Sundays and late into the nights by the light of one kerosene lamp. For once, everyone worked together without thoughts of selfish gain. The sewing shop stitched costumes without expecting a favor in return, and even Greta and A-4116 managed to be civil to each other.

On Christmas Day, 1944, everything was ready. The lights checked out, the curtain made of four blankets was in place, and the orchestra, consisting of a foursome blowing on combs covered with tissue paper, was ready. Spiess with his retinue marched in. They sat down in the first two rows of benches. The rest of the space was taken by the rank-and-file prisoners sitting at a respectable distance behind. The overture started and—out went all the lights. The power had been cut off.

With a rare show of good nature, Spiess sent out his men to bring all the kerosene lamps from the *Kommandantur*, and the show went on. The curtain opened on Zdena standing alone on the dimly lit stage, actually looking the part of the lonely soldier, standing watch with a piece of wood slung like a rifle over her shoulder, and singing the strangely appropriate lyrics from a German operetta in her husky bronze voice:

> *Have you above all forsaken me,*
> *the one who yearns so much for love.*

You who have angels in heaven with you,
send one down to keep company with me.

The orchestra watched the Germans as they blew on their combs. When Greta did her solo of a lascivious tango, Spiess sat there wetting his lips in total rapture, while the rest of the staff had expressions of absolute disbelief. The audience didn't know what was more entertaining: what was happening on the stage or in front of it. In any case, the evening was such a huge success that when it was over, Spiess ordered Greta and her crew to the *Kommandantur* and they came back with arms full of salami, bread, and pickles for the cast.

The next two evenings the lights stayed on, and the show went even better when the cast could really let loose in their native tongue. The attitude of the Germans changed subtly after this project, with Spiess dropping a remark to Mimi that he had not realized that the inmates were actually ladies, and quite pretty at that. Why, some of them could even be German women!

For a few days nothing but the show was discussed, and morale went up in spite of the foul weather and the countless daily miseries. On the afternoon of New Year's Eve, Spiess even had one of his one-way conversations with A-4116, during which he consoled her that the war would be over soon.

It won't be long now, and you will leave here. You see, our scientists have invented a new weapon. It is top secret, of course, but it is said to be a device that will cut England off from the continent.

But Sturmbannführer, what will England do? Swim to Canada?

Canada? Where's that? Anyway, once the war is over and won, you will all be resettled on a beautiful island called Madagascar. That's what the Führer said.

With this hilarious information A-4116 returned to camp to celebrate the night with her pals. She got stone drunk on nothing stronger than tap water, reinforced by another news bulletin from the Free French that was considerably more optimistic and by an unexpected event: most of the guards came to wish them a Happy New Year.

The year 1945 started with a letdown. The winter was grim, the sick line grew longer every morning, and there was the first death of pneumonia. Spiess insisted that the coffin had to be made in camp and provided a blueprint for a conically shaped chest for A-4116 to make. Her protestations that it was against Jewish law to be buried in anything but a simple box consisting of six rough planks were to no avail, and after watching her trying unsuccessfully to cut the boards according to his specifications, he pushed her away and made the coffin by himself.

Firewood was scarce and the supply limited to whatever the work details could organize among the ruins in town. Besides, the small iron stoves in the barracks did not give enough warmth even when wood was available. Everybody was constantly shivering and coughing. Many started to bring up blood. The water pipes and the latrine drain froze; the contents reached ground level and spilled over. After inspecting the stinky mess, Spiess produced a pair of hip-high rubber boots and a ten-foot iron pole and ordered A-4116 down into the muck to open the drain hole. She poked a few holes into the ice and the shit level fell, but the next morning the drain was frozen solid again.

Every other day, she went down into this stink-pit, until she smelled so foul that even from a distance, everyone who saw her coming made a large detour. Her roommates griped about having to sleep in the same room with her, but to no avail, since there was no other place to go. Kitty tried to make the others see the humor of the situation, but there was not much laughter left now. A few warmer days eventually solved the predicament.

One morning, around the end of the month, Mimi, doubled over with pain, supported by Greta, staggered through camp toward sick bay. A-4116 followed them and stood outside the door in case some help would be needed. But there was not a sound to be heard for many hours. Most of the indoor workers were unaware of the drama being enacted inside. Finally, in the late afternoon before the others returned, the thin wailing of a baby was heard.

A moment later it stopped, and about ten minutes afterward Greta and Dr. K. came out carrying a shoebox and walked toward the gate. After a short exchange with the guard, he accompanied them into the woods adjoining the camp, and sometime later all three returned empty-handed. A veil of silence descended over the event, and three days later Mimi was back at her typewriter in Spiess's office. Much later, Dr. K. said that it had been a healthy boy who could have lived.

At last a communication arrived to send a truck to another camp to receive the repeatedly requisitioned shoes. The delivery foursome arrived, and while their guard went into the office to sign the papers, they waited on a bench in the corridor of the administration building under the supervision of another soldier. He walked around with a decidedly lecherous look in his eyes until he planted himself, legs apart, right in front of them.

So you're the NEW *ones.*

New ones? What for?

Nu ja, for the brothel, of course.

Oh no, we are Jewesses and we came to get shoes issued for our camp in Neugraben.

As if bitten by a viper, the man turned his back, spat on the floor, and didn't look in their direction again. Loading some one hundred pairs of wooden sandals for five hundred inmates, the girls decided that there were certain advantages to being Jewish after all.

25

The war was going from bad to worse, and even the most patriotic Germans were beginning to have some doubts about the accuracy of newscasts, now telling them of the previously planned regrouping of their forces in order to achieve ultimate victory over the Allies. Spiess and his henchwomen were in a vile mood most of the time, and he went into an insane rage when he discovered another pregnant woman at *Appell*.

The fact that Vera, the *Capo* of Block 2, was expecting a child whose father was Benedetto,* had been known to most inmates for quite some time. Everyone hoped that Mimi's experience would repeat itself, that Greta's diplomatic skill in handling Spiess would keep Vera safe, and that maybe the war would end before the baby's arrival.

Illogically, this time Spiess flatly refused to leave bad enough alone, stood rigidly by the rules, and started proceedings to have Vera transferred to Bergen-Belsen. No separate pleadings by Greta, Mimi, or A-4116 could do anything to make him change his mind.

He only ranted and raged and accused them of trying to take advantage of his fatherly feelings for his prisoners.

A frantic search for Benedetto began, to inform him and get him to come and help Vera escape. Even a few of the guards helped in the effort to locate the Italians. He was actually found and arrived breathless on a Saturday night at the fence, only to discover that it was too late. Vera had been sent away the previous morning under the escort of the SS woman Erika, who was not a person who made deals.

Vera had been immensely popular on her block, with all of her women sharing the task of keeping her reasonably well fed during her pregnancy, accepting the coming baby as their common responsibility. Anyone replacing her was bound to have a hard time at best. The lot fell to A-4116, whom Spiess appointed in his proverbial stinginess since she was working inside the camp anyway. This way he had one more slave to send out.

The reception on Block 2 was predictably chilly when she took up her post. The first few days passed quietly. Then two SS women, accompanied by Greta, came on their regular inspection tour. In Room 2, Erika noticed that the corner of one of the ceiling planks was not flush with the rest and ordered A-4116 up on the bunk to push the plank higher to see what was above. Every inhabitant of this type of barracks knew about these low attics and the fact that they made ideal hiding places. It did not help to announce that there was nothing to be seen up there because now the bitch was up on the bunk herself and discovered a cache of provisions.

Erika ordered everything cleared out and piled on the table, to be taken on a wheelbarrow to the *Kommandantur*: a bag of potatoes, a few turnips, some flour and barley, and some half dozen glass jars with stewed fruit, plus other odds and ends that the inhabitants of the room had organized on their forays into the ruins—all now to be delivered to the Germans. A-4116 was fascinated by a jar of cherries, always her favorite. The temptation to keep them became stronger and stronger. She snatched them and managed to shove them under her bunk.

When the girls returned in the evening from work, they instantly discovered that their hideout had been looted. They descended in righteous fury upon their new *Capo*, whom they accused of having led the SS woman to the place on purpose in order to chalk up good marks with her. No protestations to the contrary helped, and Greta kept her mouth shut partly because she and A-4116 had never been great friends. Also because she resented the fact that Spiess had appointed A-4116, so to speak, over her head.

The commotion had almost died down when one of the girls from Room 2 burst into the block room with a new complaint and found A-4116 eating her cherries. This infuriated the whole block again, being proof of treason, and they embarked on a policy of passive resistance and total contempt. The truth of the matter was that A-4116 did not like what she had done either, but no one was willing to listen to an explanation, much less an apology, and although she felt guilty, she did not consider her action a capital crime.

Trouble started on Sunday when the inmates were supposed to clean up and wheel out the garbage under the supervision of their *Capos*. This Sunday they flatly refused. It had rained all Saturday, and they were sitting half-dressed on their bunks, drying their clothes by a meager fire. When A-4116 asked them to do something, they just told their *Capo* to go to hell. In itself this was not upsetting, since it made little difference whether she wheeled the garbage out six or seven days a week, but it bothered Spiess, whom she ran into on her way to the dump.

What are you doing with that garbage? That's not your job. You have one hundred and sixty prisoners to do this.

The girls came home soaking wet last night, and their clothes haven't dried. I don't mind doing this myself.

I'm not interested in all this Quatsch. What kind of a goddamned Capo are you if you can't make your people work? Demoted. Back to your old block and tomorrow out to work!

Glad to be relieved of an untenable situation, she returned to her old room, where conversation abruptly stopped when she entered. What smarted most was that not even Kitty would speak to her beyond a "How could you?" Hurt by the apparent unwillingness of anybody to listen to her side of the story, she crawled into her shell with only her notebook of letters to Mutti as a companion.

Not long afterward, Erika discovered the book during another of her inspections. Intercepted at the gate at her return from work, A-4116 was promptly whisked into Spiess's office for questioning. Since the letters were written in Czech, Mimi had to give a running translation, which she did in a very perfunctory manner, skipping the most derogatory passages.

You realize that what I'm holding in my hands is an illegal document and that it is my duty to report this and let you bear the consequences? Spiess said.

She only nodded.

Here, he said. *Burn it right now in this stove and scram.*

She opened the top of the stove, saw the flames devour her innermost feelings, and thought, *Maybe it will reach Mutti after all.*

After this incident and after Mimi's retelling of the contents of the notebook that she had read, the attitude of A-4116's roommates softened and, more importantly, Kitty became her old self again.

At the end of February 1945, the camp in Neugraben was reassigned for use by civilians who had been bombed out of their homes. The prisoners were suddenly moved to another place in an industrial section of Hamburg called Tiefstack. During the transfer on open trucks, they saw the immense extent of the destruction of the city. Rows upon rows of streets were level with the ground, with people living in the cellars of the ruins like rats, seemingly not much better off than the prisoners themselves. One look at the new camp was enough to convince anyone with eyes that this was the center of a perfect target for bombings.

The fenced-in group of four wooden barracks was framed in a web of railway tracks with two huge gas tanks and an electrical power station in its immediate vicinity. The air raids now came by day and night, with bombs exploding all around. By some miracle, the camp had not been hit yet. This was so incredible that one came to believe that the British and American pilots had exact maps designating even the smallest prisoner camp. Every night when the girls returned from work, they were astonished to find the place still intact, while everything around seemed on fire. Their admiration for the Allies' intelligence and precision knew no bounds.

26

On March 20, 1945, the sick bay, which now took up two-thirds of one barrack, was full—with almost a quarter of all the prisoners. A-4116 was lying on an upper bunk with a broken toe, due to an accident that had happened the day before: a curbstone had slipped out of her frozen hands and dropped on her foot. Next to her was Kitty, with one of her glandular fevers, when the alert sounded.

Watching from the window, they saw the guards scramble for their bunker, and only minutes later, the formations of the American bombers with their white condensation tails approached. It was really a beautiful sight in the cloudless sky, except that there seemed to be a very strong wind up there blowing their white tracks away very quickly. Just as the onlookers were beginning to worry about what this would do to the accuracy of pinpointing their targets, there was a familiar hiss and the explosion was upon them.

Thrown into the air, they landed facedown on a heap of broken bunks with the roof coming to rest on their backs. Realizing that this must have been a very close hit, they started to call the names of the other girls in the room through the noise of the continuing attack and the moans and cries of the ones trapped below. Some answered, some just whimpered, but many did not.

When the all clear sounded, rescue parties from the neighboring workplaces arrived. The roof was lifted, and incredibly, A-4116 crawled out on her own steam. The next thing she saw was Kitty, being lifted out of the rubble by her shoulders, looking like a rag-doll dredged in dust. One by one, the rest of the girls were brought out and laid on the ground. Twenty were dead, and the rest more or less seriously wounded. Zdena, the girl with the bronze voice, and Annie, the author of the whimsical fairy-tale skit—both dead. Dr. K. had a broken back and so many other injuries that she would never walk again. Only the coincidence that she had been on her rounds had saved her life.

The bomb had directly hit the treatment room at one end of the barrack. Only the girls in the top cots of their bunks had gotten away with relatively lesser injuries. The barrack was now a pile of broken lumber and glass. There was not one unbroken window in the other houses, and not one door would stay closed. There was indescribable chaos when the rest of the inmates came back from work, and had to take in the victims.

Spiess put all his men in a cordon around the compound to prevent escapes through the partly damaged fences. Even so, five or six girls managed to get away that night and survived the war hiding in the ruins of the city. Once again, A-4116 and Kitty debated the possibility of escape, but decided against it, since one was exhausted by fever and the other could not walk very well. Their coats with the yellow crosses were also a problem: without them, they would freeze. They were deep in German territory with not the slightest inkling about the direction of the front lines, and the dangers seemed to outweigh the advantages.

That night Spiess personally supervised the soup distribution. Outside it was raining and windy, and the draft constantly blew open all the doors. A-4116 was standing last in line when he shouted at her to close the door. She limped over and shut it, but two minutes later the wind had blown it open again.

Verflucht nochmal ("Damn it to hell"), I told you to shut that door, he bellowed.

Damn it, I did shut it! she yelled back.

At this, he grabbed one of the heavy earthen soup bowls and threw it at her. She ducked. The bowl crashed against the wall when she was already through the open door, and the shots from his revolver went out into the night. From now on, she kept out of his sight, stood in the last row at *Appell*, and made herself as inconspicuous as possible.

The next days were nightmares. When alerts sounded, the girls were herded into a barn that was still standing outside the compound and bolted inside, while the guards ran for cover in their bunker. A-4116 finally lost her aloofness and pleasure in air raids and was seized by abysmal terror every time the bombs started to fall. Standing packed like sardines in the barn, they were all trembling, crying, praying, or simply in a state of shock, unable to contain their bowels or bladders.

There were no more hits, but whenever they went outside, they could see that the whole city was a sea of flames. Even so, they were still sent to work every single day.

On April 5, they were suddenly lined up in the morning and loaded into freight cars to be evacuated. The train moved for an hour, then stopped in the middle of nowhere for two hours, moved again, stopped, went backward, moved again. For twenty-four hours. From time to time they were let out to urinate on the side of the tracks, covered by the soldiers with guns. Three times the train was attacked by low-flying planes. The guards scrambled for cover under the cars while the prisoners were locked inside.

During one of these stops Erna, who was a native of Hamburg, was persuaded—literally forced—by her companions to run away. She hesitated, being unfamiliar with the area, but mainly because she was loath to leave the herd. Finally, while the others created all kinds of little disturbances to distract the soldiers, she crawled away under the cars and disappeared into the night.

The following day the train reached Bergen-Belsen. There ensued a long hassle between Spiess and the *Lagerkommandant*, who refused to accept any more prisoners regardless of where the orders came from, while the train engineer refused to take them back. At last they were unloaded and brought inside the camp.

The ghoulish sight that greeted them topped anything they had seen to date.

In a quadrangle one mile long and some four hundred yards wide were forty thousand people who looked like corpses and thirteen thousand unburied real corpses. Those were strewn in heaps of about fifty to one hundred all over the place. Some sort of death dance seemed to be in progress, with one of the living dragging a dead one by the feet toward the mass graves—in slow motion, despite the shouts and kicks of the SS to hurry up. The ground in and out of the huts was crawling with lice. They formed a line—like ants—away from the corpses and toward the living.

There was no food. Water was scarce. Some people were eating dirty grass; most were just sitting or lying around, waiting to die. Some of the piled-up corpses still had a flicker of life in them. One of the newly arrived girls found her cousin with her eyelids still moving. With the help of friends, she pulled her out and incredibly brought her back to life. Asking around among the older inmates for Vera, they discovered that she had died of spotted typhus before her baby was born.

The few friends the girls did find called out to them; otherwise one could not recognize anybody. These were only skeletons covered with a gray, parchment-like skin, and eyes sunk deep in their sockets. Aside from wandering aimlessly in search of friends or relatives or for something edible, there was nothing to do but pick off each other's lice.

Still, the obligatory *Appell* was called twice a day with German thoroughness, a pointless undertaking since no one could possibly produce an accurate count anymore. People who were alive in the morning would be dead by noon. The sleeping quarters were largely empty huts, with most of the bunks having been used up for firewood. There were no pallets or blankets, and they were so overcrowded that the inhabitants had to sleep on the bare floor with their heads on somebody else's buttocks.

The typhus epidemic had started only two months before, when two cases were brought in from Hungary. There was no need for gas chambers now that people were dying at a rate of 250 to 300 per day. There was talk about cannibalism in the men's section, and considering that many corpses had a piece of their thighs chopped out, it was very probably true.

Once, there was a sudden distribution of bread rations, although the food distribution had come to a virtual standstill days before. The starved inmates sunk their teeth into the bread only to discover a strange grating sound while chewing: ground glass baked into the dough. Nobody knows how many people died of intestinal bleeding because many ate it regardless of the danger. It was not easy to think rationally anymore, being so hungry that objects and people began to double in front of one's eyes.

The SS was still putting on a show of strict discipline in their polished high boots with their whips swinging right and left, but one morning the camp woke up to discover that they had all gone, disappeared without a trace. Instead, Himmler's Hungarian SS had taken over their posts.

Naively, some of the prisoners believed that the Brownshirts would be more lenient than their predecessors, but these were absolute maniacs who shot from their rifles at anyone who came within ten yards of the barbed wire. The battlefront was coming closer all the time. One could hear the artillery all around the camp; it sounded as though they were being bypassed on all sides.

A strange new prisoner showed up in the Czech group that day. It was Sylva's friend Bubi, the SS woman from Neugraben, who arrived dressed in a brand-new striped prison shift and simply stayed, while nobody paid the slightest attention to her. On April 13 and 14, nobody left the huts anymore, because the Hungarians used their rifles the moment anyone showed her head out of the door—using it for target practice.

The door was open a crack when on the morning of April 15 one of the girls remarked in a toneless voice that there was a tank coming down the center road.

We're probably going to be machine-gunned now, someone replied.

There's a white star on the side of it, the hatch is open, and the soldiers are wearing black berets, the same girl insisted.

Go to hell with your fairy tales, somebody grumbled, but a few others, unable to resist their curiosity, crawled to the door to look. She was right. The tank was no mirage. Nor the star on its side, nor the long convoy of vehicles that followed it.

The British were finally here, the Union Jack fluttered in the wind, but the inmates were too far gone to take in the reality of it or feel joy. Hesitantly, still expecting to be shot at, they ventured out of the huts one by one. As the truth became clearer, they began to walk, crawl, and run to the fences to see their liberators close up. One after another, the armored vehicles came down the road, with the soldiers turning their pockets inside out and throwing the contents— chocolate bars, K rations, cigarettes, and other little things—over the fences and lifting their fingers in a V salutation. Many of them were crying. The things they threw immediately caused scores of bloody battles among the starved prisoners.

Somewhat later, Brigadier General Glyn Hughes made a walking tour of the camp, with his aides requesting everyone to keep calm and asking people with some knowledge of English to come forward and help with the food distribution and first aid. Tears were streaming down the general's cheeks, which he made no attempt to hide at the sight of the abysmal misery. People wanted to touch him and his men, to kiss their hands, but the soldiers had orders to keep a distance of ten feet, not being immune to typhus.

By afternoon, big lorries drove up to deliver food for distribution that the Britons had evidently found in the first German storehouse they took over. A two-pound can of meat from Czechoslovakia and a small can of condensed milk per person. Kitty dug in with her fingers and ate the contents of pork—40 percent of which was pure lard—in one sitting, washing it down with the undiluted condensed milk. A-4116 was sure she would die within hours from dysentery, since she herself was unable to force down even a mouthful.

The next day the British opened the no-man's-land between the two barbed-wire fences, making the entire compound accessible to men and women, and threw open the doors to the German storehouses. Here were several buildings with huge red crosses painted on their roofs, containing enough foodstuff and clothing to provide for an army, let alone the forty thousand inmates of Bergen-Belsen. With suicidal greed, every person still in an ambulatory state crowded into these storehouses, using the doors and windows alike. In a state of mass hysteria, people literally drowned, their heads inside barrels of pickles, mustard, prune butter, and the like, while others tried to get in over them.

A-4116 and Kitty watched the scene from the outside, feeling too weak to join the battle. But later, when they noticed their skeleton-like comrades emerging from another, less crowded storehouse, dressed up in German uniforms and boots, they ventured inside. They helped themselves to two magnificent military fur-lined greatcoats, which reached all the way to the floor, and a tent.

Thus equipped, they occupied one of the deserted watchtowers in the no-man's-land in order to get away from the lice. It did not upset them that right in front of it was a heap of corpses that seemed to change facial expressions with the different light of day or night. Nor did it bother them that the little tower was open on all sides, just a sort of balcony ten feet off the ground and very cold and drafty. After putting up the tent against the wind, they wrapped themselves in their fur coats and slept like princesses in their castle.

27

T he following days were very strange indeed. There was, of course, no way of letting the camp population simply go home while an enormous epidemic was going on. Our situation was suddenly reversed: former prisoners strolled through the camp watching SS men and women brought in to bury the dead and do all other dirty work.

Within three days they looked exactly like the inmates. Under the guard of British Tommies and groups of jeering prisoners, they were now taunted and prodded to work *Schneller, faster, you bitch, you bastard.* Bodily injury was not tolerated by the soldiers, but otherwise they thoroughly enjoyed the exchange of roles between the prisoners and their former tormentors.

Bubi's presence had been reported on the first day of the liberation. She had been arrested and was now working with the other SS women. One of the youngest survivors of the Czech group, a little guttersnipe who had grown up in camp, took a particularly vicarious pleasure in watching, and once conveyed to the British guard through a highly effective pantomime that she wanted the boots one of the SS women was wearing. It took a while for him to comprehend what she wanted, but then he gave a big grin and walked over to the woman and ordered. *Du Frau. Boots off. Stiefel*, someone shouted. *Shtee-fell, off*, he repeated, pointing with his bayonet. She finally understood and the little one walked away to the applause of the surrounding bystanders.

There were some feeble suggestions that Sylva could maybe put in a good word for Bubi, since she had really been harmless and, in Sylva's case, definitely helpful in keeping her mother above water, but Sylva was too busy flirting with the Tommies at a ten-foot distance to be bothered.

British organization of the rescue operations was a model of efficiency, and within a few days, people were not only regularly fed but an evacuation to quarantine facilities in Celle began. This was a gigantic logistical problem, because every person had to be deloused, and his clothing burned and replaced with clean garments. Thanks to DDT, nobody's hair had to be shaven. The sick had priority and were the first to leave.

One week after liberation, A-4116 and Kitty were in the first group of volunteers chosen to help with the registration and repatriation. They left Belsen on a small pickup truck with a British lieutenant and his driver and five other English-speaking freed prisoners. When they arrived on the parade square of the garrison in Celle and were helped from the truck, A-4116 fell straight into the officer's arms.

This is a very sick girl was the last thing she heard, and the next thing she knew was being in bed in a hospital ward, being asked over and over again her name and country of origin, and being unable to remember. A little doctor, herself a former prisoner recovering from typhus, examined her and said, *Sorry, girl, but you got it.*

After that, she drifted in and out of consciousness. She mustered a fierce effort to drag herself to the pail in the corner whenever she had to use the john, aware that whenever she opened her eyes, one of her companions was being carried out feetfirst, covered by a sheet. And those were always the ones who had been unable to hold their bowels and bladders the day before.

Most of the patients were delirious at one time or other, and once, one of them got out of her bed, staggered over to A-4116, and, mistaking her for an SS woman, tried to strangle her. Day after day, during the few lucid moments when the fever dropped, A-4116 tried to remember who she was and where she was but, tired out by the effort, drifted again away into another world.

After more than two weeks of twilight, she awakened in a state of absolute panic. Sitting straight up in bed, she screamed for someone to open a window, claiming that she was choking to death. Gasping for air, she was sure of hearing gunshots all around, and terrified that the Germans were returning, she insisted on getting up and running away. Two nurses and an injection finally quieted her down, and she sank into deep sleep.

28

When I woke up later the same day, the sun was shining through the windows and the room seemed different than it had been before. The girl who had tried to strangle me was smiling with clear eyes and explained in her accented German that now I would be all right, that the crisis was over. My temperature had dropped almost back to normal, and I learned that the gunshots I had heard were real: they had been fired in celebration of the armistice. It was May 8, 1945.

Very weak, but with a clear mind, I marveled at the white sheets and the cleanliness of the room I found myself in. I was the only Czech there. The other patients were all Hungarian. The doctor and nurses were mostly Polish, freed prisoners who were all immune to typhus because they had survived it earlier in Belsen. Ironically, with this mixture of nationalities, the only common language was German.

The British ran and supervised the hospitals, but did not come into direct contact with the patients. Their presence, though, was very much in evidence, and every day a cart pushed by a Tommy would appear with some delightful surprise. Cigarettes, which I could not smoke yet but kept under my pillow just to look at the picture on the package of Player's; a cake of Ivory soap; and one of my greatest pleasures: pajamas printed all over with little flowers, made in Canada. There were also other goodies like candy, chocolate, and cookies—none of which I could digest as yet. Between naps, I tried to unravel the puzzle of why Kitty had not come to visit me, fearing that she, too, had come down with typhus and maybe died. In a state of total lethargy, I pushed away thoughts of my parents and Joe, resolving to think about it later.

Every day someone came in writing down data and names of next of kin for almost everyone except myself. They seemed to include all nationalities but no Czechs. I grew very impatient because I could not understand the reason, and complained bitterly to the doctor until at last a registrar arrived one morning to whom I voiced my indignation. When I told her my name, she gave out a cry of surprise, telling me that poor Kitty had spent the last weeks poring over lists and lists of hospital inmates, trying without success to find my name. Now she was visiting one hospital barrack after another in the hope of discovering my whereabouts.

The explanation was very simple. I had been brought into the ward without identification, and put into the first empty bed available. This happened to be in a room full of Hungarians. It was assumed that I was one of them. I was, consequently, recorded only by my number, A-4116, on the Hungarian lists, which Kitty evidently didn't look at.

Now she arrived, making her entrance like an apparition from another world: her honey-blond hair in a shiny pageboy, wearing lipstick and mascara, and dressed in a pretty print dress with white sandals. All her abscesses had healed and she smiled from ear to ear, speaking in Czech.

Francinko, I thought I had lost you, and I really couldn't go home without you. I'm getting you out of here—you'll only die in this joint. I've already started to negotiate with your doctor. I have a car outside with my British factotum, and I'm not leaving you out of my sight for one more minute.

I was flabbergasted by her appearance. The doctor, who had joined us in the meantime, voiced her alarm at Kitty's idea, considering me much too weak for transportation. She warned that my diet needed to be supervised and that a relapse was almost always fatal.

Kitty would have none of it. She argued that she was perfectly capable of taking care of me, and after signing an affidavit that she assumed complete responsibility, it was agreed that she could pick me up the following day. Kitty arrived with an armful of clothes and told me to get out of my pajamas and get dressed. I flatly refused to let go of my prized sole possession that had come all the way from Canada. A little tiff ensued, but she won again.

With a warning from the doctor to take it easy and treat me with care and to feed me only small amounts of food at a time, we left in a jeep driven by a sergeant, who introduced himself as Sunshine. After a short, wild ride, during which Sunshine had to grab me at every curve to prevent my falling out, we arrived at a modern brick army barrack, where Kitty had her own room with two large, comfortable beds overlooking the garrison square.

I was put to bed, this time in a polka-dotted nightgown. Kitty left the radio on for me and told me to be a good girl, and that she would return soon. Two hours later, she found me semiconscious on the bathroom floor. Mindful of the doctor's orders, Kitty had removed everything edible to what she believed was beyond my reach, but soon after she left me alone, I started exploring my new quarters and discovered two large bowls on top of the wardrobe. With great effort I climbed a chair and ate the goulash with sauerkraut in no time at all. The result was predictable.

After this mishap, Kitty always arranged for me to have a babysitter whenever she had work to do. She recruited anyone from a fellow former prisoner up to the rank of captain in the British Army for the job. She was working as a liaison with the Repatriation Division and had a wide circle of friends. At teatime, she invariably brought along at least two or three officers, and under their combined tender loving care I began slowly to feel better.

One of them was a doctor, who suggested a rotating system of therapeutic junkets into the countryside "out of the camp atmosphere" once the quarantine was lifted. The atmosphere in the camp was anything but oppressive compared to what we had been used to, but it was a lovely thought. Our saviors showed infinite kindness, concern, and tact—never overt pity. Even though I was extremely hard of hearing and my hair was falling out in huge bunches as an aftereffect of my illness, they made me feel young, female, and attractive again.

Although Kitty and I never discussed it in so many words, we both felt a definite reluctance to go back home and face the balance sheet of the last years. At first, the quarantine was a good-enough reason for not being able to go; later, I was too weak to travel. But May became June, and though many busloads of survivors were being sent home, we made no motions to repatriate ourselves. Our friend Eva had left for Prague with the first bus and had come back with not-quite-unexpected dismal news. All our parents were dead. Joe was missing. Eva's husband was dead, and Kitty's fiancé, Ivan, had married another girl in February. Not ready to face the situation at home, Eva had come back to us and her job with repatriation.

Under these circumstances there seemed to be even less hurry to leave, especially since—at twenty-three and twenty-five—Kitty and I were having a rather good time working, playing, going to Red Cross officers' dances, and enjoying being the center of attention. The more I thought of Joe, the less I wanted to go back to him. I was seeing a lot of a young British captain who was one of my volunteer drivers and who had started to give me driving lessons.

Jason was tall and dark-haired, with the typical pink complexion of an Englishman, uninterested in small talk and a master of understatement. It took me a while to discover that what I initially took for dullness was really extreme reserve. Scratch the surface and one found the intelligence and compassion of a somewhat shy man. While out on a driving lesson, I once became frightened by a lorry entering the road and crashed into a tree. We were not seriously hurt, but still needed some attention because Jason was bleeding from a cut on his forehead and I had a gash on my knee.

The soldiers from the lorry, worried about being the indirect cause of an accident with an officer, took us to the nearest hospital—a German hospital. It suddenly occurred to me that we were surrounded only by German personnel. While I was sure that they would not harm Jason for fear of reprisals, I panicked at the idea of having a German doctor touch me. Clutching Jason's hand, I insisted that nobody could come near me unless he was present.

On our way back to Celle, Jason took my hand and said, *You will have to learn not to be afraid. These people can't hurt you anymore.* Maybe so, but just to bear me out, a few days later when we returned from a walk in the heather, we found all four tires of the jeep slashed.

29

A fter I told Jason about the news that Eva had brought from Prague, our relationship became rather close, although there were certain subjects we never discussed. The recent past was carefully avoided, so much that when we went to see a movie—*Song of Russia*, as I recall—and it was preceded by a newsreel showing the liberation of Bergen-Belsen, I watched in total detachment, incredulous about what I was seeing. One of the shots showed two girls standing in a former watchtower next to a pile of corpses, waving to the camera.

My God, that's you and Kitty! exclaimed Jason, with very uncharacteristic excitement.

Oh, no, I said, *it couldn't be.* But I was shaken.

Kitty, who had lived on the fixed idea that she would get married right after the war since she had received her one and only letter from her fiancé, Ivan, now drowned her sorrow in rounds of parties and an involvement with our friend Major Dr. Jack, whom we knew to be a married man. Romances were blossoming all over, and quite a few of our girls married Englishmen without ever returning home.

Others stayed on for different reasons. The Polish Jews did not want to return to their homeland and were waiting to establish contact with whomever was left of their families in order to emigrate to Palestine or America. The Red Cross was the meeting place of the camp, and maintained a huge bulletin board of announcements and messages from all over the world.

Among the Czechs, the people from small towns who spoke little German and had been the most assimilated of all Czech Jews were most eager to return, but many who had been brought up in German schools were unsure of the reception that awaited them. In part, this was because Czechoslovakia had started a vigorous campaign of expulsion of all German elements in the population—with the exception of the Jews, to be sure, but German-speaking Jews were by no means certain that they would be welcomed back. Even our group, which was entirely Czech, was in many cases confused and worried about just what our welcome would be like.

True enough, the representative of the Czechoslovak government, Captain Sejnoha, and the drivers of the buses who came to Celle to bring us home were urging us to come and worked tirelessly at the colossal job of getting the flock together. But in our eyes, these were idealists, who perhaps, just perhaps, were not totally representative of the general population. The mere fact that they were driving dilapidated buses, running on little woodblocks, for thousands of miles all around the Russian zone—because the Russians refused to give them transit permits—proved that they were the ones who had always been our friends. Alienated as we were and schooled in the effectiveness of six years of German propaganda, many of us were unable to grasp their outstretched hand.

For the moment, the status quo seemed perfectly acceptable even though we were still living in a military compound. We were fed, there was no rent to pay, most of our modest wishes were taken care of, and entertainment was thrown in as a bonus.

When he left Prague in 1941, Joe and I had agreed on a place to meet or send mail at the end of the war. I now wrote him a long letter in care of our friends, letting him know that I was alive, but also explaining that I had changed very much and that I did not want to return to him. Without putting the blame on either one of us, I tried to make clear that we had rushed into marriage under highly unusual circumstances and that I suspected that I was not exactly made for wedlock. I asked him not to come to Celle to try to make me change my mind, that I needed to think things through, and that in many ways I felt as if my life was just beginning and that I needed my freedom.

It was not Jason who made me write that letter, because our relationship—though close—also had a definite remoteness about it, filling a need in both of us at a given time in our lives. I did not know too much about his life in England, out of uniform, and did not ask—probably because I was not ready or able to fall in love with anybody. He, in turn, accepted me for what I was, including my long silences, and simply made himself available whenever I wanted his company.

In addition to our male friends, Kitty and I also had a protectress in the form of Colonel M.,* the South African lady who headed the Red Cross and who, for no apparent reason, had taken a great liking to the two of us. She even approved of our constant companionship with the two officers, although she was known in other cases not to be all that tolerant. She chaperoned the dances and preferred to use her matchmaking talents in favor of her own Women's Royal Army Corps. Maybe it was our facility in English that made us different in her eyes. She constantly gave us presents, took me to the dentist when I had an infected tooth, and generally mothered us.

I was much better now. My hair was growing back in little tufts, and with the parties came a renewed interest in clothes. I decided, to Kitty's delight, to make some of the beautiful Canadian beige and blue blankets into skirts and Eisenhower jackets, and was handicapped only by the fact that we did not own a sewing machine.

When we brought this problem up with Colonel M., she sent Sunshine to drive us into the country to requisition one somewhere, which he did with pleasure. We picked a nice-looking house at random in a pleasant residential area and rang the bell. A woman opened the door, and in that moment, I could see the exact same fear in her eyes that I felt when a German uniform showed up at my front door years before. When she discovered that Sunshine only wanted her sewing machine, she was so obviously relieved that she offered us thread and other supplies with it. Sunshine gave her a receipt and I went to work.

Then came the day toward the end of July when our friends

came in full force to have a heart-to-heart talk with us and a few other girls. They had rather solemn faces and had brought Colonel M. along for moral support. They told us that they were going to be replaced by new occupation forces, and that they wished for our sakes and their own peace of mind for us to return home. They suspected that the attitude of soldiers who had not been part of the liberation of Bergen-Belsen would be quite different toward us and that it would be difficult for them to comprehend the difference between a liberated Jewish prisoner and a German *Fräulein*.

This was quite true, as I had already discovered a few nights earlier when I had been dancing with a newly arrived major from Scotland. While doing the swing, he in his kilt and I dressed in US Navy pants, he remarked that he found it somewhat bizarre to have one's telephone number tattooed on one's arm. Angered by his stupidity, I had left him standing on the dance floor wondering what had made me behave in such a rude way. Colonel M. had winced and now added her voice to the convincing sincerity of the others.

They were right, of course. It was high time for us to go home. The parting was bittersweet, singly and collectively. During the following days, our liberators showered us with a trousseau of blankets, cases of soap, canned food, cigarettes, even German money. When Kitty and I were packed, we had between us thirteen pieces of luggage, plus a radio. Too much to take on the bus, and as we did not trust anybody with our possessions, we decided that Kitty would take the old sightseeing bus that was shuttling between Prague and Celle, while I would follow on a truck with the baggage in the company of three young male prisoners and the driver Pepik.

30

It was the first week in August of 1945 when these two conveyances started off toward home. The truck was an antique, and by nightfall, we had lost sight of the bus. None of the men spoke English, and our vehicle got stuck every fifty or sixty miles with clockwork precision. It was trouble enough to find the necessary fuel, but after we passed into the American zone, the mechanical problems became staggering. The American GIs could not understand why anybody in his right mind would drive a piece of junk like this and offered helpful advice—we should leave it in a ditch instead of trying to repair it.

It took all my powers of persuasion to explain that we were political prisoners going home to Czechoslovakia, which had been an occupied country for the past six years, and that most vehicles in Europe were in similar shape. Since I assumed the US Army was not willing to make us a present of one of their own trucks, would they please try and help us make ours roadworthy for the trip to

Prague? Most of the time they rose to the challenge through their mechanical skills, and treated it as they would a jigsaw puzzle.

Compared to the British, I found the American GIs amusingly naive, curious, and direct. They had no inhibitions whatsoever when it came to questions about the tattoo on my arm and propositions that could be warded off by a simple *no*. Except one, who gave advice to his buddies left and right about how to fix a disintegrating part and who turned out to be a taxi driver from New York. Intrigued by a lone English-speaking girl in the company of what must have looked to him like four hobos, he asked, *Why?* Noting that the repair job would take a few hours, he offered me his bed and affections, including some hot chocolate and Spam. My reply that I was not interested and that I was no German *Fräulein* made no impression on him, but he went on his way.

We could only drive during daylight, not trusting our vehicle (now christened Rocinante, after Don Quixote's horse) at nighttime, when it was nearly impossible to find help. We were unable to do more than some 150 miles per day at best. This left us (or rather myself) with the problem of a place to sleep. The boys never wanted to leave Rocinante unattended, and slept on top of the baggage. Every night, some attentive American noncom materialized, and offered to commandeer lodgings for me.

This sometimes led to comic situations, because I was afraid of all Germans and, if there were any around, also requested a bodyguard. South of Kassel, which we had passed through one afternoon, we had to stop, and the American sergeant on duty in the area went into the first private house to ask for a bed for me. After a lot of hemming and hawing that they had nothing suitable for a guest, it was agreed to make room for me on the living room sofa.

Sergeant Bob left after assuring me that he would be around and that I should just yell out of the window in case of need. Distrustful of my reluctant hosts, I settled fully dressed on the sofa. An hour later, the grandfather of the household, an old man reminding me of Spiess, walked in to ask whether I was comfortable. He rambled on to assure me that nobody in the German population had known what was going on in the concentration camps.

Dripping with phony pity, he started patting my tattooed arm as my panic grew with every second. Finally, I jumped up and ran to the window, screaming, *Bob, Bob! HELP!* He was inside the house in an instant, chased the old lecher away, and took me to another house on the same street, where a young woman lived with her small child. She put me next to her, in her missing husband's bed, assuring Bob that I would be well taken care of. There was something about her that made me suspect that this was not the first time she had met Bob and that, maybe, I was taking up his usual place.

On our journey through postwar Germany that summer of 1945, the vast destruction of the "thousand-year Reich" was manifest. Like Hamburg and Bremen, the large coastal ports, inland cities like Kassel and Schweinfurt were almost entirely in ruins. The members of the German population I came into contact with were, in my judgment, just as repulsive in their new servility to their conquerors as they had been in their former righteous and blind obedience to their *Führer*.

In Bad Hersfeld, we had to wait several hours for repairs. I met the commanding officer, Major Klein, a Jew from Philadelphia whose family had originally come from Czechoslovakia. Over a breakfast of powdered eggs, bacon, and Nescafé he asked me a thousand questions in his agonizing search to find a trace of his relatives. He did everything in his power to make our Rocinante capable of finishing the second half of our trip—something of a miracle since, by now, our fenders were held up by ropes and our brakes practically nonexistent. Luckily, Rocinante did not do more than thirty miles per hour, and on downgrades Pepik used to brake her by shifting into low gear. We eventually reached the Czech border near Tachov. Here we left the American zone and I met my first Russian.

While Pepik went into the guardhouse to check our travel papers, a little squat soldier with a bazooka and a red star on his cap ogled me curiously. Unable to communicate in any other language, he pointed his finger to my mouth and asked in Russian, *Ty Kurva?* (Are you a whore?) Even we understood this, and the boys on top of the truck burst out laughing. Pepik, who had returned, now informed our friend and liberator that most girls in Europe wore lipstick and that it was not necessarily a sign of loose morals.

We went on to Plzeň, where I hoped Kitty would be waiting, since she had a half sister married to a Christian doctor living in that city. But we discovered that the bus had discharged the people from this region, waited for us for two days, and left that morning for Prague, its driver believing that we must have crossed the border at another place. We unloaded the baggage marked for Plzeň and decided to push on to Prague no matter how long it would take, even though it was already dark.

From the moment we crossed the border, I had been overwhelmed by my love for the Bohemian countryside as by an avalanche, and my excitement mounted with every mile. At three a.m., on an upgrade some ten miles out of Prague, Rocinante sputtered, coughed, and refused to budge. At the end of his endurance, Pepik let out a juicy, familiar *Do prdele!* (an untranslatable Czech curse akin to *Oh shit!*) and threw himself across the cab-seat, announcing that he was going to sleep. I begged, cajoled, and offered to push Rocinante to no avail. He was already loudly snoring.

Frustrated, I walked up a few hundred yards to the top of the hill, from where I could see the aura of light over Prague while being stuck with a broken truck and a snoring driver. It just did not seem fair.

As it was getting a little lighter, Pepik woke up. After a look at my unhappy face, he opened the hood and poked around in the motor. In desperation, he gave the whole thing a violent kick, and surprisingly, the engine started. We drove into the city at five a.m., bypassing the ostensible triviality of the required quarantine and registration station, directly to the house of a former school chum of Kitty's, where we had planned our rendezvous. The whole street woke up from the noise we made as she, Jirka, his mother, and his grandmother ran down to welcome us. I was home almost exactly three years after I had left.

31

B ut was it really *home*? Here I was with three lovely people I had met ten minutes before, who fussed over food as if they had to make up for all the undernourishment we had suffered for three years in one meal, in a tiny three-room apartment that they were ready and happy to share with us.

After breakfast and a few telephone calls, we left for downtown. Like well-trained dogs, we walked back to the last car of the tram and stood on the rear platform although there were plenty of empty seats inside, not realizing that all the offensive signage about Jews had disappeared. I was to meet Max, a family friend who was married to a Christian, and at whose home Joe and I had agreed before the war to meet or leave messages.

The city was glorious in the sunshine, with relatively little damage. Since it hadn't been bombed, it looked the same as it had looked for hundreds of years—yet to me, not quite so. Stores had different names, and all these people in civilian clothes struck me as an unusual sight. I felt out of place in my cheap little cotton dress and bare legs among the still-chic, though rather dated, elegance of the late-morning crowd in Wenceslas Square.

Max looked somewhat ill at ease in his meticulously tailored prewar suit, not sure of what to say or do. First, he handed me the unopened letter I had written to Joe. My husband was dead, he said. It had never occurred to me that Joe might not survive, and a wave of shame and regret engulfed me for having written that letter. After awkwardly passing me a thousand crowns to tide me over the first few days, he invited me for dinner and, with some excuse, left.

After that, I went to the Jewish community center to find out about the process of becoming a full-fledged citizen again and about the possibility of obtaining an apartment. I did not own a single document—all my papers had been handed in three years before. I filled out endless forms, and was given a list of addresses where I might get copies of my papers. I was informed that there was a tremendous housing shortage, that single people had no right to an apartment of their own, and that families and married couples had preference. I looked through the lists of the dead and missing and the places to which they had been deported, and left so depressed that I would have taken the first bus back to Germany if that would have solved anything.

I then dropped in at my former place of business. Marie welcomed me with the same embarrassed expression as Max, immediately pointing out that nothing of mine was on the premises anymore. She had put everything in storage toward the end of the war, in the event of any accusation from the Czech authorities that she could have enriched herself with Jewish property. She also hastened to make clear to me that none of our old customers were coming to her and her husband, who was a tailor, anymore. They had refurnished the place at their own expense, and with the lease in her new name: it was all theirs.

I got the message loud and clear and left to visit Max and his family. There I was served dinner on my own tablecloth. We drank out of my mother's glasses without the slightest indication on their part that this could possibly seem strange to me. I was too embarrassed for them to comment, but did ask during our conversation what had happened to Joe's clothes that I had left with them. I didn't have much to wear for the winter and could alter some of his suits for myself.

They were telling me about the terribly hard times they had all been through and the fact that a lot of our stuff had been bartered for food when the older boy, now eighteen, came into the door dressed in Joe's suit. Alena blushed and I quickly reassured her that it did not matter, that I understood, and that the suit looked better on Jarousek than it would on me anyway. But I did *not* understand. Not then and even less when the same scene in different variations repeated itself over and over in the next few weeks.

There were, of course, many others who had an entirely different reaction to my return, but it was difficult to shake off the initial bitterness. I went to a small town to visit a former customer of ours, with whom my mother had left a certain amount of money and her diamond earrings. My mother had made this client's wedding dress, and now she, her mother, and her husband welcomed me like a long-lost child. They gave me triple the sum that was due to me, maintaining that money had lost that much of its value, and they did not want to let me leave. Having no children of their own, they even came up with the idea of legally adopting me. I appreciated their good intentions, but found it impossible after a few days to accept the idea of living in a small town with relative strangers.

There were others who invited me to their houses and fussed over me, trying to arrange my life and always a little uneasy about inadvertently hurting my feelings. I came to hate the clichés that I was being drowned in.

How you people could survive is a miracle!

Nobody before the war had ever referred to me as *you people.*

I also heard, *You have no idea how much starvation we had to suffer here. Everything was on coupons!*

And, *A pretty, clever girl like you will get married again in no time, and all your problems will be over.*

These phrases and dozens more like them infuriated me, and I found I could relax only in the company of my surviving friends from Terezín. Some of them who had returned early after liberation were living in apartments confiscated from the Germans. Others were again living in their old homes, especially if they had owned the building, although very often without a stick of furniture. With these friends, at least, I did not feel apologetic for my existence. They tried to cheer me up, assuring me that I would adjust, that things had a way of falling into place—and, by the way, why on earth had I taken so long to come back? All things considered, we were alive, and what else did I want?

That was obviously true, but for the first time in six years, I felt drained of all my energy, confused, tired, and hopelessly alone. Now it was Kitty who pushed me to do this or that, to collect my possessions, to go out, to do something—that is, when she found the time in her growing social life.

She had come up with a place to stay for the two of us with the family of her former boss, who had a large, underutilized apartment on the Old Town Square facing the monument of Jan Hus. They offered us a room under the assumption that Kitty would eventually marry the forty-five-year-old bachelor who had been in love with her ever since she started working for his firm as a teenager. He had been waiting for her to grow up for years. He had even been imprisoned for two years, after being caught leaving the ghetto after one of his clandestine visits to Kitty and her parents in Terezín. For the time being at least, we had a roof over our head.

Unlike Kitty, I was incapable of responding to the kindness and concern of people, yet desperately lost without their company. The bureaucracy was driving me crazy. It took weeks to get copies of my documents. I was offered a job as a multilingual assistant with an export firm, attractive because it would entail immediate travel. When I applied for a passport, it proved necessary, in addition to my other papers, to provide proof of my registration as a Czech national in the census of 1930. After a wait of two weeks, I received a slip of paper in the mail, with the information that my father had entered *German* as his and my nationality. Disgusted, I tore up the official notification, which prevented or held up the issuance of a passport, regardless of the fact that I was a Czech citizen, born in the Czechoslovak Republic, and had been ten years old at the time of the census. I later substituted proof of my schooling in French schools, which were considered the equivalent of a Czech education, but by then the job had been filled by someone else.

I had no motivation to look for another job and no desire to reopen my old business. Having no financial worries, with a little money, a government pension, and few expenses, I just drifted along. Walking the streets for hours, I imagined my parents on every familiar corner. The only place that could lift me out of this melancholy state was Smetana Hall, the home of the Czech Philharmonic. Music was the only language that had not acquired a double meaning for me.

Meanwhile I went out with a number of different men, hating to have to sit at home and stare into an empty room. I got involved in some quite impossible situations. I was seeing entirely too much of a married man, a former friend of Joe's whose mother had been in Terezín while he, married to a Christian girl and the father of two technically Aryan children, had survived comfortably in Prague. He had become obsessed with the notion that his dead mother had wanted him to marry me, because she had once said—years before, when I was introduced to her as Joe's fiancée—that I was the kind of girl he should have married. I was completely indifferent to his intentions, but also to the feelings of his wife, who tried to commit suicide when she discovered where and with whom her husband spent most of his time. Evidently, her mother-in-law's pronouncement had been a bone of contention in many a marital argument, the implication being that he should have married a Jewish girl.

Finally my old friend and visitor from Terezín Dr. V. put an end to this nonsense, of which he was highly critical, by announcing that I was his mistress, which was quite untrue at the time. There was also a Slovak partisan with long hair and a dashing mustache à la Stalin, who titillated my bent for the mysteries of the underground but who turned out to be more stupid than heroic. And there were a few old flames I had carried a torch for when I was sixteen and had considered very interesting.

After a few dates, these idols usually proved to have clay feet, but mostly, their minds seemed to operate on an entirely different level from mine. They belonged to different political parties and everybody wanted me to join theirs. All I wanted to join was the human race.

Under President Beneš, who had returned to Prague from exile, we had a coalition government, including a fairly strong Communist Party. Its ranks were swelled by many of the returned prisoners, who had nothing to lose except their freedom, once more a fact that many did not seem to realize. After the betrayal at Munich, there was a feeling among many of my generation that only Communism could avert a recurrence of fascism. I spent whole nights listening to these arguments, particularly among artists.

My own opinion had not crystallized, yet I argued that the Communists would only substitute the bourgeoisie for the Jews in another totalitarian system. I stayed clear of any commitment, never having been a joiner. Our entire social situation was still quite abnormal, with inflation rampant, the continuing housing shortage, and the generally low work morale. I, for one, was so conditioned to being ordered what to do that I was incapable of any initiative. The prospect of having to go to some official place to obtain a document made me tremble with fear of and contempt for whoever was in charge. *Authority* had become a dirty word. My characteristic self-discipline had fallen by the wayside around my time in Bergen-Belsen; I found neither money nor possessions worth working for.

Back in Celle, at the suggestion of Colonel M., I had given the Red Cross a list of names of my relatives who had fled in the early days of the persecutions, though I didn't know where they had found refuge. These lists were posted at embassies and consulates in most cities of the western world. It was in this way that my cousin Peter Sachsel discovered that I was alive.

When his first letter arrived, I felt a happy shock. Peter was special. We were both born in 1920 and had been playmates up to the age of five, when he moved with his parents to Bratislava. But we visited often, and Peter's father, Emil Sachsel, my mother's favorite brother and my favorite uncle, was an even more frequent visitor when he came to Prague on business. The last time I had seen Uncle Emil was in 1939, before I got married. He had noted how happy he was that Peter was in Lyon. Peter had left to study in France before the German invasion. Unable to return and not foolish enough to try, Peter had made his way via Cuba to the United States in the hope that his parents and little brother would follow.

By the fall of 1945, when I saw Peter's return address in the United States, I had given up all hope of ever hearing or seeing anybody from my family again. As I read his letter, I could well imagine his joy when a friend informed him that the Czechoslovak Consulate was looking for him, mixed with the disappointment that he must have felt when he discovered that it was only I who was seeking him instead of his parents or brother.

The Sachsels—Peter's parents and younger brother—had been deported from Bratislava, and had vanished in the death machines of Eastern Europe without a trace. During our correspondence, it became painfully clear to me that Peter could not face coming back to Czechoslovakia, if only to claim his property, although I desperately wanted to see him. Like me, he apparently was trying to put the recent catastrophic past in a locked box and start anew. This plan was, of course, easier to resolve upon than to carry through, since the memories and questions of why one had been spared in the general slaughter stubbornly refused to go away.

32

With fall came the bad weather and the devaluation of the Czech currency. The first curtailed my aimless wanderings through the city; the second reduced my cash reserves to one-tenth of their value. Our savings accounts were frozen, although some money could be released in emergencies for returning prisoners. I still had my pension, but this put me on a tight budget.

Partly for this reason, but mostly to kill the time I couldn't walk the streets anymore, I took a job. It offered no challenge, bored me to death, but paid quite well, mainly because my new boss was flattered to have the previous owner of a rather well-known firm as his employee. During that time, I ran into our former customers, who, after first inquiring about the fate of my mother, asked me how soon I planned to reopen my own business. They had not bought any new clothes since I left, and thought it a shame that I was working for somebody else. I, in turn, shied away from the red tape

involved in any restitution, the return of licenses, and the responsibility for employees.

Eventually, I did go see the erstwhile contents of the salon at
their place of storage: a half-open shed. The Louis XIV furniture
was mildewed and fell apart at the slightest touch. There was, naturally, not one inch of fabric left, nor any other supplies, these
having been used up by Marie. Only the machine heads were still
usable because they had been heavily oiled.

Starting over again just seemed like too much of an effort. Still,
one of our old clients who had also been a good friend of my mother's kept at me with dogged tenacity, arguing that Mutti would not
like my loafing and indecision at all. She countered all my protestations by offering me a studio adjoining her place of business.

Claiming that she had the political leverage through the Communist Party to get the restitution of my license moving, I let her go
ahead, assuming correctly that, even so, it would take months before anything concrete would materialize. My lack of enthusiasm
must have been exasperating to her, but she put me in contact with
a gentleman who sat on the commission dealing with the return
of Jewish businesses. He declared himself willing to help—in return
for my dead husband's ski boots—even though I did not belong
to the Communist Party. Every commission had four members,
each representing a political party of the government coalition, and
worked in this "I'll do you a favor and you do me a favor" way.

When nothing happened for several weeks, my man informed me
confidentially that there was a tremendous backlog of applications
and that the tendency was "not to hurry with the restitution of Jewish

businesses." I never discovered whether this was only the Communist viewpoint or characterized the entire commission. However, it was clear that the German occupation had left a legacy of anti-Semitism, albeit of a much subtler and hidden kind. This was also apparent in the Union of Liberated Political Prisoners, where a very fine line was drawn between repatriated Jews and Christians.

This, though, did not seem to affect the general population, as attested by the hundreds of new mixed marriages, aside from marriages of returned widows and widowers. However, many of these people decided very soon that life without their families brought too many bitter memories, and that the official emphasis on our liberation—by the Russians—did not bode well for the future. These people started emigration proceedings, preferring to raise their children in countries in less vulnerable geographic positions.

I did not succumb to either the marriage or the emigration fever. In the first case, I had made a firm resolve never to marry again after what I considered the fiasco of the first time. And I felt an incapability or perhaps a fear of getting deeply attached to any other human being. In the case of emigration, no matter how I assessed my immediate situation, whatever roots I had were in Prague. I still believed in the basic decency of the nation, particularly with Beneš as president and the extravagantly loved and admired foreign minister, Jan Masaryk, representing the Czechoslovak Republic in the United Nations.

These two symbols of the prewar state were "building bridges to the West," and many of us were convinced that they would be successful, that the political situation would stabilize, and that the strength of the Communists would deflate. Colonel M., who had remained in touch with me by mail, floated the idea of my settling in South Africa in one of her letters. She noted that I did not seem happy in my native country, but I thought that what I heard about hers was too much like anti-Semitism. I pushed the suggestion aside.

Increasingly I began to feel like fair game for every man I encountered, a situation that I perhaps unconsciously encouraged out of my need for human warmth. It seemed like I was expected to pay for every dinner or theater invitation with a night in somebody's bed—and, moreover, feel flattered in the process. To counteract this state of affairs, I went out and bought a puppy, a wirehaired fox terrier similar to my murdered Tommy. I took it with me everywhere, even to work, where it dotted the establishment all over with little puddles, to the dismay of the customers but tolerated by my boss, who in any event only put in an appearance once a week to collect the receipts. My own therapy worked only too well. I became overly attached to this soft little creature and afraid that, somehow, it would come to harm if I kept it. On the spur of a moment, I gave it to my boss's children as a present.

One day I had a call from an old friend from Terezín, acting as an intermediary for our friendly gendarme Karel, who was too shy to dial my number himself, requesting a meeting. I arrived at the restaurant we had agreed upon and was looking for a policeman in uniform, when a slight blond man in a navy suit with a pearl in his tie got up to greet me. We sat down, followed by some awkward moments of surprise at our changed appearances and positions.

In answer to his questions, I gave him a sketchy account of my adventures. Somewhat later and hesitantly, he came out with his motive for asking for this rendezvous. He had heard that my husband was dead, and that made him think that, well, maybe we could go out together and that, maybe, if it worked, he blushed, we could one day get married. He was dead serious, and in good Bohemian country tradition, he hastened to assure me that I would be well taken care of. He had left the gendarmerie and bought himself a farm so large that he had to use hired help to work it.

There was no need for Karel to tell me that he was well-off; I had already noticed the large diamond ring on his finger. *Jewish property* flashed through my mind, but I kept quiet. Karel had, after all, helped a great many people and had been more than kind to me. His proposition, though, struck me as totally incongruous, even though I knew a former denizen of Terezín had married "her" gendarme right after the war and was already expecting a baby. Not wanting to hurt Karel's feelings, I told him how surprised and honored I was by his proposal but that I had decided never to get married again.

When he objected to such an obviously rash resolution at the age of twenty-five, I told him that the whole subject was academic anyway because, legally, I was not free. This was true. It would take six months to issue an official death certificate for my husband after I found an eyewitness to his death, and longer if there was no proof. Karel's parting words to me were, *I'll wait; meanwhile we can still be friends.*

I had found out from Karel that Honza had returned, and was

now in a state hospital suffering from tuberculosis. Considering that Honza was only in his early thirties, I was glad to hear that he was alive and let a few weeks pass before I went to see him. When I finally did, I was shocked to find him in the terminal stages of the disease, with no hope for recovery. He managed a feeble smile when I took his skeletal hand, and could barely talk through a racking cough that seemed to bring up all the blood left in his emaciated body. Why, why did this brilliant and good man, who would have had so much to contribute to humanity, have to die now when it was all over? Why was destiny so capricious, always destroying the best among us? Tormented by these thoughts, I slipped into uncontrollable crying spells like the ones I had not been able to shake after my parents left Terezín.

As if on cue, I found Margot sitting in the waiting room of a doctor we had both gone to see with various complaints. Weeping, we fell into each other's arms, almost instantly recalling the prophecy of the old woman in the ghetto. Margot had completed her years of captivity in Mauthausen, in Austria, where she had been found near death by a Czech colonel, himself a prisoner for close to six years. Although she was a citizen of Germany, she wanted to return to Prague, where she hoped to find Arthur. Colonel S. offered to use his influence to obtain temporary permission to do so. When Margot arrived in Prague, she discovered that she was a widow. Arthur had died in one of the death marches in the last weeks of the war.

Margot moved in with friends and determined never to return to Germany. She had initiated emigration proceedings for the US, where a brother of her dead husband's lived in Cincinnati. She had a long waiting period ahead because of the complicated American quota system, made more difficult by the temporary nature of her Czechoslovak residency permit. Monthly renewal was mandatory and annoying. When we met, she was having a liaison with Colonel S. that had evolved out of gratitude for his help in getting her back into Czechoslovakia. He was a Jew and, by a strange coincidence, was the one able to tell me the details of my husband Joe's odyssey.

When Joe was brought to the Small Fortress near Terezín, he was put into a cellblock with jailed officers of the Czech army. When these prisoners were later moved to Auschwitz, he was sent with them, losing by some oversight of the jailers his designation as a Jew. This was not even discovered in Auschwitz, largely because his mother had refused to have Joe circumcised but also because his name did not sound Jewish. The prisoners in his group considered him and Colonel S. as two of their own and never gave the Germans the slightest hint that they had Jews among them. This way Joe escaped being a candidate for the ovens.

As the eastern front neared, these prisoners—regarded by the Nazis as hostages—were evacuated to Mauthausen, where conditions were similar to Bergen-Belsen. I was told that Joe wrenched out the gold caps of his teeth to sell them for bread because his legs were swollen to triple their size with hunger edema. By the middle of March there was a call for volunteers for the salt mines in Ebensee, with the promise of higher food rations. Against the age-old maxim of the military to never volunteer for anything, Joe swallowed the phony bait and went.

He died inside the mines around the time that I had been liberated in Belsen. It seemed as if he had always dared and courted death at the same time. With him, his entire family was wiped out, as if they never existed. I had known for quite some time that my husband was dead, but the details now put the stamp of finality on it. Until then, I had, irrationally, always expected that he would walk through the door one day with a big grin and a wild story of some improbable adventure.

It was different with my parents. No matter how many people I talked to and how many questions I asked, I could not find one surviving person from their transport. Their destination was listed in the official documents as Riga, but that could mean any number of smaller camps in that area. Contrary to all common sense, I simply could not believe deep down that they were gone forever. I knew it, yet would not convince myself of this reality.

Kitty and I still lived together in the same apartment, but were growing apart more and more as the need for the physical protection of one another diminished. Except for a few common friends, our circles were rather incompatible. I leaned more toward the company of artists and intellectuals, whereas Kitty preferred the moneyed, pleasure-loving crowd that tried to recoup their prewar way of life as fast as possible.

Kitty refused to speak to her former fiancé, Ivan—even on the phone—so the task of collecting her belongings from him fell to me. When I went to see him, I could not suppress a sarcastic question: why had Ivan written such a glowing love letter, a letter that would have done honor to a great poet, in December and then married another girl in February? It seemed to me that with the information available in Prague, he must have known that the war was drawing to an end and that he could have at least waited until Kitty's return.

To this, he could only say with visible embarrassment that it was none of my business, but that he had thought that Kitty was so incurably ill that it would have been madness to think that she could ever become the mother of his children. This conviction must have been very strong, because the clothes he now returned to Kitty had already been altered to his wife's size without the bother of even having them dry-cleaned.

In November 1945, after three months living in the apartment of Kitty's boss and his family, their pressure to set a wedding date began to grow. An argument ensued, during which Kitty declared that she had never been officially engaged to her boss and that, in any event, she had no intention of getting married—now or in the near future, to him or anybody else.

After this we had to move in somewhat of a hurry.

Kitty went to stay with a distant relative of her father's, who had a studio apartment, with room only for one. I was stranded for a few weeks accepting hospitality here and there, some afternoons not knowing where I'd spend the night, when good old Dr. V. offered me his place for a few months while he was substituting for an ailing colleague in a provincial town. The apartment had been his own before the war, and he had succeeded in getting it back, but the furniture was gone and it contained nothing except a few suitcases used as coffee tables and a folding cot. Grateful to have a roof over my head, I bought a couch and moved in.

Actually, Dr. V.'s filling in for a colleague was more of a flight from Prague than a necessity. I had first met him in Terezín as a client of Joe's mail service. He had been engaged to a Christian girl, his former operating room nurse. He was, at the time, an almost legendary figure in the ghetto for his steadfast fidelity to his fiancée, and had to endure many a ribbing for this medieval devotion. As his confidante I had listened to unending songs of praise about the character of this golden lady. Moreover, Dr. V. was an assimilationist who carried the idea to the extreme. He claimed that the only salvation for the Jews lay in their disappearance into the general population, citing the marriage of his favorite aunt to a well-known Czech painter. He also thought that Jewish women were too possessive of their men.

No sooner had he returned to Prague than it was brought to his attention by the hospital grapevine that his beloved had been living for three years with an SS officer. This German man had been an administrator of the hospital and, in fact, had been arrested at her apartment. At first, Dr. V. dismissed the information as malicious gossip, but finally confronted Jarmila with these allegations. Her side of the story was that she had been forced into the relationship with the German under threat of imprisonment or worse.

Deeply hurt and unsure of the truth, he retreated into work and his empty apartment, while continuing to see Jarmila on and off. This was the state I found him in when I returned to Prague. I listened to his agonized searching for a workable solution and realized that he was in love with his own concept of Jarmila, which had no basis in the real person. In the end, Dr. V. decided to let intelligence and magnanimity win over his wounded feelings and give her another chance. As it happened, the mind was willing but his body revolted: ergo, the escape to the provinces.

The apartment was a mixed blessing, as his absence deprived me of my favorite escort to concerts. I had become very fond of Dr. V., mainly because—like most alumni of the camps aged closer to forty than twenty—he had had a firmly established set of values in place at the time of our incarceration; he had barely been vulgarized or corrupted by the experience. This was certainly connected with one's stage of life at the time. My own faith in people was greatly shaken, and I had become somewhat of a cynic.

In the music of Gustav Mahler, I discovered a sort of mirror image to my own state of mind, vacillating between violent spurts of energy, hope for the future, and deep despair. I wanted very much to be the independent, self-sufficient, free woman. Yet I kept casting around for a fatherlike figure to keep me from foolish escapades, often not trusting my own judgment. The masculine side of my nature, always present and encouraged by my father, had become much stronger during the years of captivity, when I had played the role of protector for Kitty and lived and worked like a soldier in the field or worse. It showed itself in my gestures; even my voice had become much deeper than before.

For the first time in years I was now living entirely alone in the sometimes ghostly quiet of my new quarters. At times I enjoyed my solitude, but it also invited incessant rethinking of the past. Somewhere along the way, I had acquired the notion of a certain complicity in the murder of my parents that I found myself incapable to reason away. I had kept my promise to survive through sheer luck and willpower, but this was not enough to allay my self-reproach of not having done more to save them. Yet I did not know at all what I could have done.

Christmas drew near, and my pride made me refuse several invitations, considering them like bones thrown to a hungry dog. Snow had fallen and I eyed my skis and boots—among my few possessions that had been returned to me—standing in a corner. I toyed with the idea of escaping to the mountains from the city filled with memories.

On New Year's Eve, I spent a few hours in the place I felt most comforted when depressed: a hot bathtub. A little mouse emerged from a hole in the wall and slowly made her way toward me on the rim of the tub. Lost and undecided which way to go, she seemed a symbol of my own existence. We stared at each other for quite a while, and then she decided to return to her hole. Suddenly I felt this as the last unbearable loss and fled the apartment, intending to go to a party after all. But instead, I started to walk through the passageways of the old city toward the river and down to the lower embankment, which used to be a sort of lovers' lane in spring and summer, and where I had my first kiss some nine years before.

I arrived at a recess in the river wall with a step to the water and a large iron ring for tying up boats. Suddenly I had a vivid memory of being five years old and on my way home from a gym class with Mademoiselle. That day, for the first time in my life, I had seen a drowned man fished out of the river and tied to that boat ring. He must have been in the water a long time, because he was all green and slimy, and reeked of dead fish and decay. I had pushed my way through the legs of the curious onlookers to the front and had stared at the figure for quite a while before my governess realized that this was not the most suitable sight for a little girl.

In a nightmare the following night, I had confused the drowned man with the Waterman, a legendary figure in Czech folklore who lures innocent girls into the depths of the water. I had often been threatened by the maids that he would come get me if I misbehaved. Twenty years later now, that image was alive again. He was calling my name and telling me how dark and soft the water was. I stood there transfixed, staring at my beloved river with its slowly moving ice floes, remembering how often I had skated not far from where I now stood, and how I had loved to go swimming in summer on the opposite side. The water looked cold yet peaceful, with the reflection of the streetlights dancing on it like little stars.

I felt a hand on my shoulder. A white-haired policeman said, *Miss, this is not a good place for a midnight walk alone. It's too cold for that. Tell me where you live; I'll walk you home.* As if awakening from a dream, I let myself be led away and dropped exhausted into my bed.

The next morning was New Year's Day, 1946. I woke up with a clear head, packed a bag, took my skis, and caught the first train to the mountains, arriving in the late afternoon. The following day I took the gondola up to the summit, worrying a little about how good a skier I would be after a break of six years.

On top, the mountains were decked out in their most festive finery. The sky was cloudless and the pine trees were heavily sugared with new snow. There was not a soul around to take away the sudden intimacy between myself and the universe. Awed, I looked at the miraculous beauty surrounding me, as if especially created for my welcome. If there was a God, I felt His presence here, as well as gratitude for being alive. I buckled on my skis, and whistling the last movement of my favorite Brahms symphony, I schussed down the hill.

Franci and her mother, Josefa Rabinek, August 1922

Franci (*left*), age three
and a half in 1923 in Prague,
with her cousin Peter

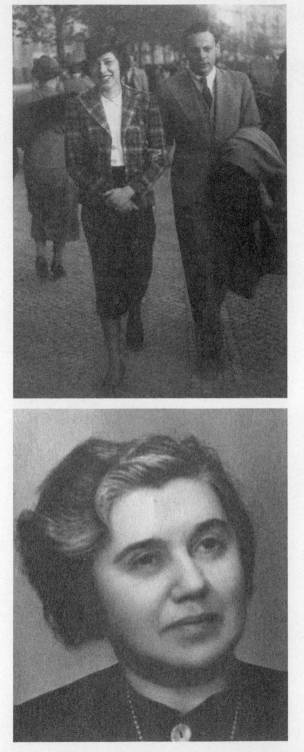

Franci and her architecture student boyfriend, Leo Oppenheimer, in Prague, May 1937

Last photo of Josefa Rabinek, Franci's mother, 1940

Emil Rabinek, 1930s

Marianne Golz, Franci's
cellmate in Pankrác prison,
in June of 1939

Franci and Joe
Solar wedding
photo, 1940

Joe Solar with
dog Tommy

Gisa, 1939

Franci (*left*) and Kitty with a
British soldier in Celle, 1945

Red Cross Colonel Margaret Emmeline Montgomery (*seated*)
with other British personnel in Celle, summer 1945

Franci (*left*) and Kitty
after liberation in Celle,
summer 1945

Franci and Kurt Epstein wedding photo, December 21, 1946, Prague City Hall

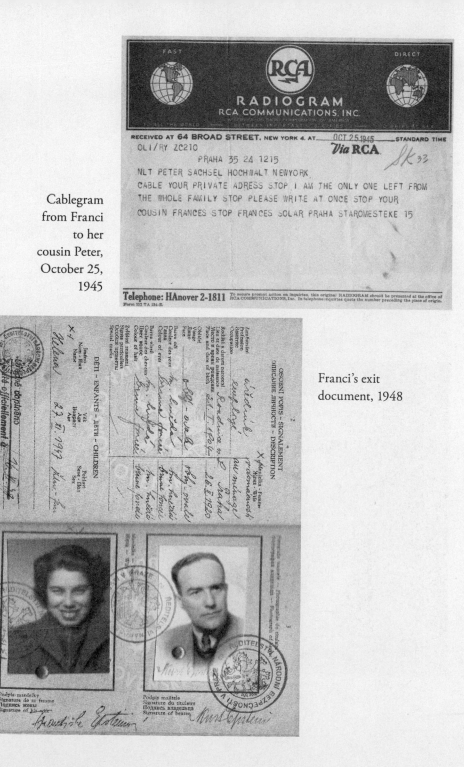

Cablegram from Franci to her cousin Peter, October 25, 1945

Franci's exit document, 1948

Margot Körbel in Israel, 1951

Franci, dress designer in New York City, 1955

AFTERWORD

I n the spring of 1946, Franci Solar set about assembling the documents, premises, and staff with which to open her new salon. She wrote to her cousin Peter, now in the American army, to send her fabrics, and the latest *Vogue* and *Harper's Bazaar*. She was planning to rest up at a spa in Slovakia in August before opening in the fall. Then, in July, she wrote him that she was getting married.

> *It all happened very quickly, actually all in one week . . .*
> *His name is Kurt Epstein . . . He's forty-two years old, a*
> *head taller than I am and very good looking (he's a well-*
> *known athlete, a swimmer, and related to the Petschek*
> *family). I've known him since I was twelve, when he was*
> *our trainer at the swim club and I hated him with all my*
> *heart because he was so obnoxious to us teenagers that I*
> *always thought of him as an awful, arrogant person. And*
> *all of a sudden Mr. Epstein wasn't obnoxious at all.*

Kurt Epstein had been one of the one thousand Jewish men deported to Terezín in December 1941. Terezín had been his military garrison when he was a reserve lieutenant in the Czechoslovak Army, and Kurt was soon appointed one of the camp's eight quartermasters. Unlike Joe Solar, he was the antithesis of a black marketer; he worked to ensure that the food he distributed actually arrived in the mouths of the prisoners it was intended to feed. His parents were deported to Auschwitz in the same transport as Franci, but they had been murdered there. Like Franci, Kurt had been selected by Dr. Mengele for a forced labor camp, and he was the sole survivor of his family.

> *He's a wonderful person who holds rather old-fashioned views of women,* Franci wrote to Peter in September, *which is good because he behaves with a certain honorableness that younger men don't have. He also loves me—which does not blind him to my faults. It's in every way the opposite of my first marriage, where my husband idolized me and let me do all kinds of stupid things. In the end I only hated him for his weakness and lost my last bit of respect for him. It looks like Kurt won't make this mistake and will keep a certain authority. It helps that he's sixteen years older than me. You know, my girlfriends are the happiest about all this. I was always such an "enfant terrible" and everyone who knows me is glad that finally there's someone who won't let me dance around his head.*
>
> *As far as finances go, Kurt makes enough money but I want to have my own business. I don't feel good when all I have to*

think about is a household. Also one never knows what will
happen and it would be madness to abandon my clientele. I
would be terribly unhappy at home and Kurt knows that I
have too much energy for my life's achievement to be dusting.

Kitty begged Franci to marry Kurt, even though he was not her usual type. Other friends thought she was making a mistake. He was a provincial, who fell asleep at concerts and, despite all his prowess as a swimmer, didn't ski. Franci's best friend, Helena, later told me that she thought Kurt would be a good husband but didn't believe Franci was in love with him. He spoke nothing but Czech, and had no street smarts.

They married on December 21, 1946, in Prague's City Hall and, after taking out a mortgage on the Epstein home in Roudnice nad Labem, bought an apartment in Wenceslas Square. Franci opened her salon at 20 Old Town Square. She wrote to Peter that she now employed seven seamstresses, was planning a trip to Paris to see the collections, and that Kurt was earning a good salary working for a fellow survivor's company. He was also coaching the national water polo team, and was a member of the National Olympic Committee. And . . . she was expecting a baby.

Dear Uncle, Franci wrote on January 9, 1948, *I've become*
a totally besotted mother . . . Helen will have a nurse but
she isn't here yet, so for the moment I'm doing everything
myself. For the time being, the baby doesn't need much and
no one can breastfeed her for me anyway. I need the day to

have at least thirty-six hours. But I definitely like this role of mother and have already decided (with the father, of course) that we'll have more . . . I still like to go to the theater or go dancing but the fact is that when I go, I worry whether my little girl isn't crying at home. It's a good thing I'm breastfeeding since the scarcity of milk is catastrophic.

January was Czechoslovakia's last month as a democratic state. The scarcity of milk was due to a drought, exacerbated by Soviet policies, that had put Czech agriculture in crisis. The coalition government was also in crisis. The Communist Party organized mass demonstrations, and a Soviet envoy arrived in Prague. On February 25, President Edvard Beneš appointed a new Communist government.

There is no letter to Peter documenting my parents' decision to emigrate. The family story is that Kurt surveyed the armed militia marching in the streets, called them "Nazis in different-color uniforms," and vowed that he would not make the mistake of remaining in his country twice. Franci argued that she was not going anywhere. She had just turned twenty-eight. She had just re-created her salon. She had a three-month-old baby. For the first and only time in their marriage, my father slapped her.

Furious, Franci stalked out into the cold. Then she returned. Any doubts she had about emigrating were dispelled on March 10, when the body of Jan Masaryk, the hope of the democrats, was found in the courtyard below his office in the Czechoslovak Foreign Ministry.

Thousands of Czechs fled immediately. Fortunately, Kurt Epstein had applied for an American visa in 1945, when he returned from the camps. In March 1948, during a trip to France with the national water polo team, Kurt telegraphed his cousin, Franzi Petschek, in New York. She had married into the banking family that had evacuated their family members and employees on a special train in 1938. The Epsteins had been invited to leave Czechoslovakia on that train but had decided to remain.

My parents flew out of Prague on July 21, 1948, with two suitcases and me in a canvas bag. Franci wore all the clothing she could. Along with diapers, she packed the Epstein and Rabinek family photographs and three porcelain figurines that had belonged to her mother.

Whenever I asked about her arrival in New York, Franci replied that it had been over a hundred degrees, the flight had taken twenty-six hours, and of the ten dollars they had each been allowed to take out of the country, the New York Port Authority had taken eight. The Petscheks settled them in the Hotel Colonial, across from the planetarium on Manhattan's Upper West Side. She never mentioned any feelings.

Franci's friend Helena Slavíčková had predicted that Kurt Epstein's sports reputation would not travel if they emigrated, and that Franci would wind up supporting the family. She was right: Kurt Epstein spoke no English. He could not find a job. The Petscheks did not believe in hiring relatives. There was no demand for water polo coaches in Manhattan and few swimming pools.

Franci turned for help to her Prague obstetrician, Dr. Karel Steinbach, who had also emigrated and was now the hub of Manhattan's

Czech community. Within two weeks, Dr. Steinbach sent her a fashion client: Czech soprano Jarmila Novotná, who was singing at the Metropolitan Opera and needed a dressmaker. It was illegal to work in the Hotel Colonial, so Franci found a cheap basement apartment, bought a sewing machine, and once again started sewing.

My parents had a very difficult first decade in the United States. Although Franci often pointed out that her Manhattan Czech social circle was far more interesting than the one she had had in Prague, she had serious medical problems. For most of the 1950s, she was the breadwinner, cook, household manager, mother, and wife. In 1951, she had a difficult birth with my brother Tommy. The family's financial situation was precarious: my parents juggled the monthly rent and salon creditors, trying to maintain a middle-class style of life. After nearly starving to death in the camps, my parents insisted on eating meat every day. Franci also insisted on attending concerts and the theater. In 1956, she had a nervous breakdown, serious enough to warrant extended, intensive psychoanalytic treatment. Her cousin Peter, who was now earning a good living as a chemist, helped pay for it.

Kurt slowly learned English and took intermittent menial jobs. He was a devoted father, but hopeless in the kitchen or around the house. Like Franci's father, Emil Rabinek, he helped his wife by doing the bookkeeping for her business. Eventually, he was able to join the International Ladies' Garment Workers' Union and worked in a factory as a cutter in Manhattan's garment center. In 1960, the Epsteins' third child, David, was born.

During the 1950s and 1960s, Franci exchanged letters with her sister survivors—Kitty in Prague, Margot in Jerusalem, and others in Israel, North America, and Australia. Occasionally, I would meet one of them in our living room. Then, in 1964, after a protracted and painful legal effort, Franci received reparations money from the German government and used part of it to visit the two women with whom she had been in the war: Kitty and Margot.

Since 1948, Kitty had been living in a tiny apartment in the center of Prague with her husband and son. A social butterfly even in the gray Communist world, Kitty modeled herself on Hollywood starlets, and dyed her hair blond. She, too, was the sole survivor of her family. She married Kurt Egerer, a fellow survivor with whom she had a son. She worked as a multilingual secretary, using her German, French, and English, first for an export firm and then for the Chief Rabbi of Prague. After her husband died, she lived with her Czech Protestant boyfriend, who shared her joy of life. She spoke very little about the war, she told me when I visited Prague, but the scars she carried were not only from the boils she had developed in Hamburg.

Margot, who was living with my parents in Wenceslas Square when I was born, had difficulties of another kind. She had been liberated at Mauthausen and returned to Prague with a Czech colonel who had been imprisoned there. But as a former citizen of Germany, she was not welcome in a Czechoslovakia that expelled its Germans. She emigrated to the newly established State of Israel in 1949, where she met a Berlin-born survivor named Bier. The two lived, improbably, in an old Arab house on the premises of the French convent in Jerusalem's Ein Karem. Bier was the nuns' handyman and chauffeur to the director of the Israel Museum. Margot worked in a dress shop for a few years and never had children, but served as my surrogate mother while I was a university student in Jerusalem. During that time, she told me a great deal about her relationship with my mother during the war.

The sisterhood of Czech Jewish survivors remained in close touch. They exchanged news about their current lives as well as war stories—who had done what to whom and what that meant after the war. They discussed the televised hearings of the Eichmann trial in 1961. They talked about every war movie they saw, including *Night and Fog* (1956), *Judgment at Nuremberg* (1961), *The Pawnbroker* (1964), and *The Shop on Main Street* (1965). And they also discussed books.

Franci was probably the best-read among her friends. She had attended French, German, and English schools in Prague and was familiar with the classics in all three languages. She also loved the Russian writers. Every Sunday, she read the *New York Times Book Review* and ordered whatever interested her from the New York Public Library. She loved the novels of Vladimir Nabokov and, of the survivor authors, most admired the work of Primo Levi.

I don't know if she read Olga Lengyel, Gisella Perl, and Vladka Meed, women survivors who published their books in the late 1940s, but I do remember her buying Czech survivor Zdena Berger's autobiographical novel *Tell Me Another Morning* in 1961. Then, in 1964, the *Times Book Review* reviewed a translation of Ilse Aichinger's novel *Herod's Children*, based on her experiences as a half-Jew in Vienna during the war. Recognizing the characters, Franci discovered that her cousin Ilse had become a famous Austrian author. She wrote to her and reconnected with the Viennese branch of the Rabineks—now scattered throughout the world—who assumed Franci had been murdered in the war. Over the next decade she told and retold her wartime experiences to them.

I don't know when Franci began thinking about writing her own book. Perhaps she never stopped thinking about the notebook of letters to her mother that she had written in Neugraben and had been forced to burn page by page. In the mid-1950s, she retold many of her camp experiences, first to an antagonistic German doctor assessing her wartime injuries for the purpose of monetary reparations, and then to a sympathetic American Jewish psychoanalyst. In February 1974, she retold her story—in chronological sequence— for the William E. Wiener Oral History of American Holocaust Survivors, a then-unique project that audiotaped two hundred testimonies. She was just short of her fifty-fourth birthday.

That validation of her experience may have been the impetus for Franci to finalize her memoir. She titled it *Roundtrip*, a sardonic reference to the route she had taken through the Second World War from Prague to Terezín to Auschwitz to Hamburg to Bergen-Belsen to Celle and back to Prague. In a now-dated preface that she titled "Explanation," Franci wrote:

> Why do I feel compelled to add my voice to the great chorus of statistics, learned reports, psychological studies as well as more or less successful treatments in fiction and drama already written? There is no one answer, but perhaps

my first and foremost concern is with my children and their generation, who seem to me almost as troubled as I was at their age. They are prone to deep exasperation about the status quo, and to flight into drugs. My daughter, of course, asked me questions from the time she became aware of the tattoo on my arm, and has never stopped, a fact perhaps brought about by the natural identification of a girl with her mother. My sons never showed much interest, getting almost visibly uneasy or bored when the subject came up in conversation.

Since children tend to be strangers to the inner life of their parents and their motivations and reactions, and having no fortune to bequest, I can only try to give them an honest and true picture of their mother in her youth and of my way of dealing with the perplexities of existence. It might give them some understanding of the diversity and often puzzling behavior of the human animal, in addition to the dreadful corrupting force of power in the hands of a few individuals, who usurped it with the help of an indifferent, intimidated, and dissatisfied population.

The deciding factor was a trip to Colorado where I was visiting friends whose ancestors had settled the West. I found myself in the company of a group of young people far removed from the experience of anyone with my background. Having studied twentieth-century history in college and disturbed by the staggering facts of World War II, they plied me with questions about how it had felt from the inside. Uninhibited by the delicacy of their elders, they convinced me that here was a generation who really wanted to know what had happened to me, so that they could perhaps relate it to their own experience. Like my own children, these young people were desperately trying to find their own raison d'être in a world still full of injustice, violence, and oppression. They were engaged in various forms of political protest, draft evasion, or escape from reality. The thought occurred to me that if my own contemporaries, particularly in Germany, had voiced their doubts and opinions more intelligently and forcefully, we could have possibly been spared the terror and mass annihilation of the Hitler era.

In 1973 and 1974, when I think Franci was finalizing her memoir, Germany was still two countries divided by the Berlin Wall. President Richard Nixon was struggling to stay in office in the aftermath of Senate hearings into the Watergate scandal. The civil rights movement, the war in Vietnam, and the women's movement had deeply polarized America. In Israel, the 1973 Yom Kippur War had once again raised the issue of Jewish (and Margot's) survival. Franci and her customers talked about all these subjects during fittings. Some of them were themselves refugees with similar backgrounds. Some were Americans with little connection to Europe or Jews.

As had been the case in Prague, Franci was her customers' confidante and they were hers. All knew she had survived the Second World War in the concentration camps. Some preferred not to discuss it, but none could avoid seeing the Auschwitz tattoo on her forearm. Her favorite client, Marya Mannes, a prominent journalist who had put Franci in one of her books, may have encouraged Franci to write down her story. Another client, literary agent Cyrilly Abels, sent it to publishers in 1975. It was rejected by every one.

In the mid-1970s, many American Jews—and I would bet some of the editors Cyrilly pitched—wanted to distance themselves from concentration camp victims. Holocaust studies courses at universities and Holocaust centers were still in their infancy. Not until 1978 would the term *Holocaust* become publicized through the internationally popular television miniseries. Although the U.S. Holocaust Memorial Museum later became the most visited museum in Washington, it would not open until 1993. And although second-wave feminism was growing in the United States and Jewish women were among its leaders, the movement had not yet made much of a dent in the Jewish community.

In its attitude, language, and content, *Franci's War* was far ahead of its time. With the exception of Anne Frank's posthumous diary, Holocaust literature in the United States was dominated by male writers, particularly Elie Wiesel—then the prototype and spokesman for the thousands of victims who were coming to be called "survivors." Few male memoirists in the Jewish community wrote much about women's lives during the Holocaust. It was a non-Jew, William Styron, who published *Sophie's Choice* in 1979—and that novel was about a Polish non-Jewish survivor. In Israel, largely due to the sensationalist novels of Yehiel Dinur (who wrote under the pseudonym Ka-Tzetnik, the Hebrew abbreviation for "concentration camp prisoner"), Holocaust survivors were viewed as damaged goods. Czech-Israeli author Dita Kraus, who accompanied Franci on most of her wartime route, told me that even the great Israeli statesman David Ben-Gurion allegedly said, "Every man who survived was a *Capo*, and every woman a prostitute."

Franci focused almost entirely on the experiences of women in her text. In addition, she viewed her wartime experience through the lens of a highly assimilated Prague Jew and proud Czechoslovak citizen. Neither she nor her parents were religious. She did not speak Yiddish. Moreover, Franci wrote candidly and dispassionately about sexuality and love, including homosexuality and sexual barter. She knew how potentially damaging and even dangerous that was in the early 1970s, because she disguised the names of those women whose sexual choices she describes.

Not many writers are able to separate rejection of their work from rejection of themselves, and Franci was no exception. The rejections of her text wounded her and confirmed her suspicion that no one was interested in her experience. She gave the manuscript to me, to use as I saw fit. After all, she said, I was the professional writer in the family.

The last thing I wanted in 1975 was my mother's book. I had lived with it all my life. It was her story, not mine. I wanted to get away from, not into, it. Even though I was then in my late twenties, I had neither been able to rebel against my parents nor truly leave home. I was in the process of writing my own book, *Children of the Holocaust*, in an effort to separate what was mine from what was hers. My book, about the intergenerational transmission of history, trauma, and resilience, was published in 1979, and it was emotionally complicated for us. We never discussed it explicitly, but I felt that while Franci was proud of her journalist daughter's first book and enjoyed participating in its promotion, she felt that her own experience had been overlooked. She began to speak about her war experiences at local venues, but she did not pursue the publication of her memoir and neither did I.

In the spring of 1989, Franci experienced a brain aneurysm, went into a coma, and died without being able to speak to any of her children again. Over the next seven years, as my own form of mourning, I researched her and her maternal ancestors' lives for a book that became *Where She Came From: A Daughter's Search for Her Mother's History*. In it, I traced three generations of dressmakers in Central Europe and drew on *Roundtrip* as a source for the section about the Second World War. After I finished that book, in 1997, I filed away the memoir with my other research materials and focused on my own work.

Over the years, I had often been asked to help write or translate other survivor memoirs, and sometimes, when I was particularly interested in the subject matter, I agreed. Together with the author, I retranslated Heda Margolius Kovály's memoir *Under a Cruel Star: A Life in Prague, 1941–1968* from the Czech, and it became an important college text. I translated part of Vlastá Schönová's Terezín memoir *To Be an Actress*, and worked with Paul Ornstein on *Looking Back: Memoir of a Psychoanalyst*. I also wrote introductions to the work of two Canadian survivors. I was sent so many manuscripts about the Holocaust to read and review that I had to refuse almost all of them in order to do my own writing.

During the last twenty years, however, I have tried to keep up with the work of feminist-influenced scholars researching the experiences of women in the Second World War.

Then, in 2017, a friend alerted me to the existence of a videotaped testimony my mother had made in 1985 for the Fortunoff Archive at Yale University that neither my brothers nor I knew existed. In October of 2017 my family obtained a copy and watched it for the first time. That same month, the *New York Times* and the *New Yorker* both broke stories of Harvey Weinstein's sexual abuse of employees and associates and the international #MeToo movement hit the headlines.

After watching Franci's videotaped testimony and sharing it with friends, I reread my mother's text, and recognized it as an important primary source. Several of the people Franci describes have become famous or infamous since the 1970s; some can be found on Wikipedia. They include not only Josef Mengele, but Franci's well-informed Pankrác cellmate, Marianne Golz; Jewish prisoner Lotte Winter (Franci's Sylva); and Nazi guard Anneliese Kohlmann (Franci's Bubi). Spiess, the Nazi who forced her to burn her journal, was tried by the British for war crimes; his real name was Wilhelm-Friedrich Kliem.

I discussed the idea of publishing Franci's memoir with my two brothers. We agreed that she had wanted her book to be published, and would want us to get it published for the seventy-fifth anniversary of her liberation from the camps. We agreed that I should do minimal editing and offer it to publishers in Europe, Israel, the United Kingdom, and the United States. Franci would be pleased to know that it was bought first by Ikar, a large Slovak publisher, and Mladá Fronta, a large Czech publishing house.

Nothing in my mother's book—including the heterosexual and homosexual relationships and acts of sexual barter—came as a surprise to me. I had heard the stories, met many of the people, and knew some of them—Kitty, Margot, and Peter—very well. Unlike many Holocaust survivors, Franci was never reticent about her experiences—if anything, I believe she told me too much too soon. My brother Tommy refused to learn Czech or listen to the survivors who conversed in our living room. I chose to listen but adapted Franci's psychological defense of dissociation for myself. I heard the words but refused to understand what they meant.

It was not until I myself had spent almost a decade in psychotherapy and wrote my own memoir, *The Long Half-Lives of Love and Trauma*, that I felt able to address *Franci's War*. I grew up in awe of my brilliant, candid, and pragmatic mother: awed by what she had lived through and impressed by the lessons she drew from it. A dropout from two elite high schools in Prague (a German gymnasium and a French lycée), Franci often referred to the camps as her "university," where she had received a unique education in human behavior.

In her "Explanation," Franci wrote:

> An American doctor once asked me, after discussing the irreparable damage to my nervous system, whether I hated the Germans.
>
> I do not, mainly because I feel that hate is a sentiment I can ill afford, since it ultimately leads to the hatred of one's

self. I certainly cannot hold the people born after 1930 accountable for what their parents did to me and my family, but every German older than that makes me decidedly uncomfortable, as if the blood of my dead companions were still on his hands.

I do resent greatly the publications of books by former Nazis and the buildups these receive.

I do resent the meager rehabilitation payments the present regime makes to its victims, determined by courts where the accused has become the judge, and hampered by bureaucratic red tape which leaves thousands of cases unresolved years after the war, as if waiting for the victims to die before a settlement of their claims is made. While the considerable restitution payments to the state of Israel show a certain goodwill and wish to make amends, the sum total of German reparations can never even partially make up for the devastating material and psychological damage done to their victims. Try as I may, I cannot find any reason to admire the nobility or basic justice of the German dealing with this problem.

My feelings toward them are best characterized as indifference mixed with pity for my German contemporaries and their elders. Just how does a father of a German son or daughter answer their questions? Can he sit down and give an honest account of his actions during the Nazi era without feeling his ears burn? Where were the voices of the intelligentsia, the great artists and humanitarians of the golden period in Germany's cultural past? How is it that one is hard put to find a German who will admit ever having been a member of the SS or Nazi Party? Could the infernal plans of the leaders really have been carried out without the cooperation or at least tacit approval of the vast majority of the population?

The trial of Adolf Eichmann, like the Nuremberg judgments before, left me without any sense of satisfaction or revenge but only with the bitter aftertaste of futility. Necessary as they may have been.

I could not care less about what happens to this divided country or its separated families in the East and West, and refuse to join in the shedding of crocodile tears over their fate.

I do consider it a supreme irony of history that West Germany is today so much better off economically than England, who held the fort for so many years alone, and that Germany is courted from all sides as an ally against the Communist Bloc.

All this, though, does not add up to hate—more to a curiosity whether there, in fact, exists a new Germany. Could this new Germany withstand another mass hysteria to "Follow the *Führer*" if another madman arose in another disastrous economic depression, with a need for a scapegoat?

My greatest concern is the possibility that due to human nature, it could happen again in a different form, under different circumstances, anywhere in the world.

EDITORIAL NOTE

E diting *Franci's War* posed several challenges. My brothers and I assume Franci must have written at least parts of her memoir by hand, before 1974, but we found no manuscript pages among her papers after she died in 1989. Her memoir was typed on an English-language typewriter, on the thin onionskin paper that she used for airmail correspondence. Her will makes no mention of the memoir or her wishes regarding it.

The typescript is corrected in Franci's handwriting or crossed out with typed *X*s. Nevertheless, there are grammatical errors, missing words, typos, misspellings (Osveczin instead of Oświęcim, *Sturmbandführer* instead of *Sturmbannführer*), run-on sentences, and very long paragraphs. The narrative is not divided into chapters, and punctuation is inconsistent. I made corrections and broke the narrative into chapters. Page 2 of Franci's typescript is missing. I used the gap to move the Rabinek family history ahead several pages.

Franci presented some key quotes, conversations, and letters within quotation marks, left others unpunctuated, and chose to translate the entire text of a love letter she received (in Italian)!

Had a publisher accepted and worked with her on the text in the 1970s, Franci would have had the opportunity to look over the text, correct errors, and discuss her narrative decisions as well as her sardonic title: *Roundtrip*. But her unexpected death of a brain aneurysm at the age of sixty-nine in 1989 made all of that, as well as the decision to publish in 2020, impossible.

While my brothers and I are certain that she would have wanted her memoir to be published, we are less certain about other matters, starting with the author's name. Our mother wrote the book as Frances Epstein but we feel that in 2020, she would have preferred to be Franci Rabinek Epstein, especially since the *Stolpersteine* (memorial stumbling stones) laid for her and her parents in the center of Prague bear that name.

Because there were multiple corrections required to update her original preface, I decided to quote from it in the afterword rather than to insert my own voice into her narrative. I (and the copy editor) did minimal line editing.

It was relatively easy to check and correct dates. Names, however, presented a challenge. Franci used the real names of her cousins Kitty, Vava, and Peter but created pseudonyms for other people—I assume that she did so to protect the privacy of her sister prisoners and their families. I marked all pseudonyms I recognized with an asterisk and left it to scholars to identify them. Franci also used the pseudonym "Buchwald" for the forced labor camp of Neugraben, one of eighty-five sub-camps of Neuengamme. In reality, there was no forced labor camp named "Buchwald," and it is unclear why she used that name.

In another perplexing reference, Franci names "Ilse Koch" as the female commander at Auschwitz who inspected her group of Czech Jewish women inmates before they were sent to Neuengamme. I think that my mother was aware that Ilse Koch (known as the "Bitch of Buchenwald") was not the woman she encountered in Auschwitz. Franci may have been using the name "Ilse Koch" figuratively, or she may have confused her with Irma Grese, another sadistic Nazi female commander who was in Auschwitz. I eliminated the name.

Forty-five years after Franci wrote her memoir, largely due to the internet, I was able to check many facts that were unavailable to her at the time.

In March 1993, Gunter Buck, then a thirty-seven-year-old teacher in Hamburg, contacted me. Buck was researching a former forced labor camp in his neighborhood when an Israeli interviewee told him that Franci had been a prisoner there and that her daughter had written about her. I gave Buck permission to quote from my book, *Children of the Holocaust*, and he provided me with many details of my mother's time in Hamburg for the sequel, *Where She Came From: A Daughter's Search for Her Mother's History*. He identified "Spiess" (the German word for "Sarge") as Wilhelm-Friedrich Kliem. Born in 1896, Kliem was a master carpenter conscripted into the Wehrmacht, an SS guard at Auschwitz, then the commander of Neugraben. He was tried for war crimes in 1946 by a British war crimes tribunal in Hamburg and sentenced to fifteen years in prison.

University of Warwick Professor Anna Hájková, a scholar of queer Holocaust history, women, and sexuality, has definitively identified "Bubi" (1921–1977), the female SS camp guard at Neuengamme, as Anneliese Kohlmann and the prisoner my mother named Sylva as Lotte Winter. She also put me in touch with Alyn Beßmann, archivist at the Neuengamme Concentration Camp Memorial, who sent me a copy of Franci's registration card in Neugraben. Given this documentation, I replaced "Buchwald" with Neugraben in the text.

In 2018, Ronnie Golz, who read about Franci's time in Pankrác prison with Marianne Golz in 1939 in *Where She Came From*, sent me photographs and his website for Marianne (1895–1943). She was his father's first wife.

In preparing *Franci's War* for publication, I queried the Facebook group Jewish Genealogy Portal and was sent documentation of Franci's Aunt Hella (Helena Sachsel, 1883–1944); her Terezín adoptee Gisa (Gisela Kauffman, 1932–1944); and her Red Cross protector Colonel M. (Margaret Emmeline Montgomery, 1901–1993), who was a sister-in-law of Field Marshall Bernard Montgomery and is warmly remembered in the recollections of at least three other Holocaust survivors.

Finally, my brothers and I are very fortunate to possess original prewar family photographs. Many descendants of Holocaust survivors have none. Our mother's and grandmother's customers of Salon Weigert in Prague are responsible for their survival during the Nazi occupation of Czechoslovakia. After the Velvet Revolution of November 1989 (which Franci did not live to see), I was able to obtain additional photographs and documents from the

Jewish Museum, the Museum of Decorative Arts in Prague, and the Terezín Memorial. Because Franci and Kitty worked as interpreters for the British Army in 1945, Franci was given several photographs taken by the British that summer. Her cousin Peter Scott saved her telegram of 1945 and all her postwar letters and returned them to me in 2015.

Helen Epstein
LEXINGTON, MASSACHUSETTS

ACKNOWLEDGMENTS

Many friends, family members, and colleagues helped bring *Franci's War* to publication. I'm especially grateful for the early and enthusiastic encouragement of scholars Dr. Michael Berenbaum, Dr. Atina Grossmann, and Dr. Betsy Anthony in the US; Dr. Zoë Waxman and Dr. Anna Hájková in the UK; Dr. Kateřina Čapková and Dr. Arno Pařik in the Czech Republic; and Gunter Buck and Alyn Beßmann at the Neuengamme Memorial in Hamburg.

Elisabeth Benjamin, Jean Hearst, Susan Kahn, Irena Klepfisz, Susan Hecker Ray, Rochelle Rubinstein, Sandy Fong-Ging, Joelle and Leon Gunther, Ilse Browner, and Tom Manoff provided valuable early support. Franci's sister survivor Dita Kraus, who accompanied Franci from Terezín to Celle and has written her own memoir, was kind enough to read and fact-check Franci's.

For help in documentation, I thank my brothers Tom and David Epstein; our cousin Karel Ehrlich; and the resourceful members of Facebook group Jewish Genealogy Portal, especially Kaye Prince

Hollenberg and Doron Leitner, who identified Franci's Terezín "adoptee" Gisa Kauffman.

I thank my imaginative and indefatigable agents, Kristin Olson in Prague, who brought *Franci's War* to the attention of Czech and Slovak publishers, and Carolyn Savarese in Boston, who brought it to Penguin in the US and to Michael Joseph in the UK.

My husband, Patrick Mehr, adored his mother-in-law, and was involved in every step of bringing her memoir to publication. He never once doubted its value. My writing partner, Helen Fremont, was also essential every step of the way.

Lastly, I thank the warm and professional team at Penguin, who made the publishing process a pleasure: Kathryn Court, Victoria Savanh, Bennett Petrone, Bel Banta, Kate Hudkins, and the many others whom I did not meet but who contributed to the creation of this book.

Readers who would like to see and hear Franci may access her videotaped Holocaust survivor testimony at the Fortunoff Archive at Yale University.

TIMELINE

October 28, 1918   Establishment of First Czechoslovak Republic following the collapse of the Austro-Hungarian Empire.

November 11, 1918   Armistice signed to end First World War.

February 26, 1920   Franci born to Josefa and Emil Rabinek in Prague.

January 30, 1933   Adolf Hitler is appointed chancellor of Germany; first German concentration camps established in March.

March 12, 1938   Germany annexes Austria in what is called the "Anschluss."

September 30, 1938   The Munich Agreement enables Hitler's annexation of the Sudetenland (parts of Czechoslovakia with a predominantly ethnic German population).

March 15, 1939   Hitler enters Prague and annexes the rest of Bohemia and Moravia; appoints Konstantin von Neurath as Reichsprotektor. He quickly abolishes Czech political parties and trade unions, and institutes the Nuremberg racial laws for Jews.

June 1939	The Rabineks are arrested by the Gestapo and are interned for two weeks in Pankrác prison.
September 1, 1939	Germany invades Poland; Second World War begins.
April–June 1940	Germany invades Denmark, Holland, Belgium, and France.
August 1940	Franci Rabinek marries Joe Solar.
June 1941	Germany invades the Soviet Union.
September 1941	All Czech Jews ordered to wear a yellow star.
September 1941	Hitler replaces Konstantin von Neurath with Reinhard Heydrich as Reichsprotektor.
October 16, 1941	First deportation of Czech Jews to Lodz.
November 24, 1941	First deportation of Czech male Jews, who transform military garrison of Terezín into a concentration camp.
May 27, 1942	Operation Anthropoid: Czech and Slovak Resistance fighters assassinate Heydrich.
June 10, 1942	Hitler orders reprisals for Heydrich assassination. The villages of Lidice and Ležáky are targeted and 1,300 Czechs, including 200 women, are murdered.
August 1942	Joe Solar is deported to Terezín and works on the new rail line connecting the camp to Bohušovice station.

TIMELINE

September 1942   The Rabineks are deported to Terezín; Franci remains there, but her parents are sent to Maly Trostinets, now Belarus, where they are shot to death.

September 6, 1943   5,007 Jews are deported from Terezín to Auschwitz II-Birkenau. All are tattooed and registered into the Czech Family Camp.

December 1943   Kitty is deported to the Czech Family Camp at Auschwitz-Birkenau.

March 1944   Joe Solar is arrested and imprisoned in the Small Fortress, the prison of the Prague Gestapo in Terezín.

March 8–9, 1944   3,700 prisoners of the Czech Family Camp gassed to death in Auschwitz.

May 1944   Franci Solar deported to Auschwitz-Birkenau as part of large transport to lessen crowding at Terezín before visit by the International Red Cross.

July 14–16, 1944   Franci, Kitty, and their group of 500 mostly Czech women deported from Auschwitz to Dessauer Ufer in Hamburg.

July 20, 1944   Attempted coup against Hitler fails.

September 1944   Franci's group moved to Neugraben, where Franci works as an electrician.

January 27, 1945   Auschwitz liberated by the Russian Army.

February 3, 1945   Massive US air attack on Berlin.

February 1945	Franci's group moved from Neugraben to Tiefstack.
February 13–15, 1945	Allies bomb Dresden; Hamburg was subject to extensive strategic bombing by the Allies from 1943 to 1945.
April 5, 1945	Franci's group moved to Bergen-Belsen.
April 15, 1945	British Army liberates Bergen-Belsen; Franci and Kitty are moved to Celle one week later.
April 30, 1945	Adolf Hitler commits suicide during Battle of Berlin.
May 4, 1945	General George S. Patton's army enters Czechoslovakia; Patton and British prime minister, Winston Churchill, advocate Allied liberation of Prague, but Allied supreme commander in Europe, General Dwight D. Eisenhower, accepts Stalin's demand that the Red Army liberate the city.
May 5–6, 1945	Prague Uprising by Czech Resistance; German Luftwaffe bombs Prague.
May 8, 1945	Victory in Europe Day (V-E Day): Allies formally accept Germany's unconditional surrender.
August 1945	Franci and Kitty leave Celle to return to Prague.

NOTES ON THE
CONCENTRATION CAMPS

Terezín (in Czech) or **Theresienstadt** (in German) was a
former military garrison town sixty kilometers north-
west of Prague that the Nazis turned into a unique combination of assembly point, transit camp, and ghetto in November
1941. Some 148,000 Jews were transported to Terezín, most from
Bohemia, Moravia, and Germany, but also from Austria, the Nether-
lands, Slovakia, Hungary, and Denmark. The majority were immediately or eventually deported to extermination camps. More than
33,000 people died of illness and/or malnutrition in Terezín. Among
its prisoners were some of the most prominent Central European Jewish artists, performers, philosophers, rabbis, writers, and educators.
Terezín was controlled by the SS, guarded by Czech gendarmes, and
administered by Jews coerced into executing Nazi policy. Touted in
Nazi propaganda as a "model ghetto," it had a vibrant cultural life
and schooled its children. On June 23, 1944, after a deceptive beautification effort by the Nazis, an International Red Cross team was

invited to inspect the camp and fell for the ruse. Their report helped discredit accurate accounts of Terezín and other Nazi concentration camps. Terezín was liberated by the Soviet Army in May 1945.

The Czech Family (or Theresienstadt) Camp, also known as BIIb, was a sub-camp of **Auschwitz-Birkenau**. On September 6, 1943, 5,007 Jews from Terezín were transported to **Auschwitz-Birkenau**, tattooed, registered, put behind electrified barbed wire, but not shaved. They were allowed to keep their clothes and their children, who were housed in a children's barrack. Their papers were marked "special treatment" and "six months." The mortality rate was no lower here than in the rest of Auschwitz, but as in Terezín, the children received somewhat better food and were taught by teachers. After six months, those who had arrived in September 1943 and were still alive were murdered. As they went into the gas chamber, they sang the Czechoslovak national anthem, "Kde Domov Můj" ("Where Is My Home"); the Jewish national anthem, "Hatikvah"; and "The Internationale."

In December 1943 and May 1944 (Franci's transport), freight cars from Terezín brought 12,500 more prisoners to **Auschwitz-Birkenau**. At the beginning of July 1944, some (including Franci's group) were selected to work in forced labor camps. The remaining (nearly 7,000) prisoners were gassed to death. The killings of the Czech Family Camp inmates in March and July of 1944 constitute the largest mass murder of Czechoslovak citizens during the Second World War. Of the 17,500 prisoners sent to the Czech Family Camp, only 1,294 survived. Kitty and Franci were two of them.

Dessauer Ufer was part of the Neuengamme network of Nazi concentration camps in northern Germany that consisted of a main camp and more than eighty-five satellite camps. Tens of thousands of people from across occupied Europe were imprisoned there, including French, Italian, and Russian POWs and slave laborers, and Jews. At least 42,900 people died inside the Neuengamme camps, on the death marches when the camps were evacuated, during bombings, or after they were transported to other concentration camps.

In mid-July 1944, a transport of 1,500 mostly Czech Jewish women left Auschwitz-Birkenau, including Franci. Five hundred of them were sent to Dessauer Ufer, near Hamburg's oil refineries, to clear the rubble caused by Allied bombings. In September 1944, those five hundred were moved to Neugraben. In February 1945, they were moved to Tiefstack. In the first week of April 1945, they were moved to Bergen-Belsen.

Bergen-Belsen was a concentration camp located in northern Germany, established in 1940 to house prisoners of war. It came to include Jews, political prisoners, Roma "asocials," criminals, Jehovah's Witnesses, and homosexuals. Late in the war, it became a dumping ground for thousands of Jews driven from other camps on death marches. Approximately 50,000 people died in Bergen-Belsen, including Anne and Margot Frank. Poor sanitary conditions and lack of food and water led to starvation and an outbreak of disease. Franci contracted typhus, but there were also outbreaks of tuberculosis, typhoid fever, and dysentery. The British Army liberated the camp on April 15, 1945. More than 13,000 former prisoners died after liberation. Franci and Kitty recuperated in the town of Celle, eleven miles away, where the British Army set up a hospital. Because of rampant disease, they later evacuated and then burned down the camp.

Children of the Holocaust

Conversations with Sons and Daughters of Survivors

"An enormous achievement, heart-wrenching and unforgettable." —*Chicago Tribune*

CHILDREN OF THE HOLOCAUST

Conversations with Sons and Daughters of Survivors

HELEN EPSTEIN

WITH A NEW INTRODUCTION

The daughter of Holocaust survivors, Helen Epstein traveled from America to Europe to Israel, searching for people with one vital thing in common: their parents' persecution by the Nazis. Epstein interviewed hundreds of men and women coping with an extraordinary legacy. In each, she found shades of herself.

"A passionate, brilliantly illuminating work."
–*Los Angeles Sunday Times*

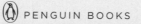 PENGUIN BOOKS